The Great Deception

American Christianity

Don Britton

ISBN 978-1-64416-131-9 (paperback)
ISBN 978-1-64416-132-6 (digital)

Christian Faith Publishing, Inc.
832 Park Avenue
Meadville, PA 16335
www.christianfaithpublishing.com

New American Standard Bible
Please note that any print in red in this book is Scripture directly used from the New American Standard Bible.

Printed in the United States of America

Dedication

This book is dedicated to all the good and decent true Christians who have been misled by the modern teachings flooding the church today through all the false shepherds who are using their position for the unjust gain of money, power, and the approval of man rather than for the approval of God. These are men who look after their own best interest rather than that of the people they are supposed to serve. May this book be an eye opener for you and may you find the truth that sets you free.

Don Britton
Christianmyths.org@gmail.com
www.Christianmyths.org

Contents

Foreword

I grew up with just a little Christian influence. My mother and grandmother would take me to a community church on occasion. There I was introduced to some facts about the Bible and God. Mostly Sunday school stories about Noah and the flood or Jesus dying on the cross for our sins. Since I grew up in the fifties and sixties, there was still some spiritual Christian influence in the public schools. Most teachers had a Bible on their desk and often referred to the Scriptures when moral questions or issues came up. When I was a young boy, these influences had an impact on me for the good, and I was very tender-hearted during those years. But I was not born again at that time.

When I got into my teenage years, I was soon influenced by the world and my own desires of the flesh. As a result, I began to be immoral with young women. This pattern became an obsession and ruined my first marriage and was carried on into my second marriage. When I was thirty-two, my second wife (my current wife) told me that she was done with me and told me to leave. Even though my heart was hardened through many years of sin and rebellion to God, I remembered those early years of hearing about Jesus and came to the conclusion that the only hope for me was in God. So one Saturday in late 1979, I called on God in the privacy of my home and in the back-bedroom closet. I was broken into tears with deep regret over my sin and wasted life. I cried and cried out to God to forgive me and to give me a new beginning. I had heard from someone about being born again and getting to start all over. I repented, and the Lord met me that day and I promised Him then, that I would do whatever He showed to me to do and I would also tell others about Him. I quickly lost all my worldly friends and my life was suddenly changed. My wife took me back, and we both began a journey of walking with the Lord together. Soon we were going to church.

I assumed that the church would be filled with righteous, holy, godly people. I felt so unworthy to be in the presence of such godly people. But it did not take too long before I discovered that the church had a lot of people practicing sin and some were committing adultery like I used to. There were also liars, pretenders, gossips, and a number of other sinners showing up in the church; and I was troubled by all this. So we changed churches and it didn't get any better. Over a period of three years, we went to a Charismatic church, a Baptist church, a Presbyterian church, Kay Arthur's Reach Out Ranch, various Bible studies, various revivals and various other "Christian" seminars and I began to feel very discouraged and confused. I almost turned away from the Lord by my third year as a Christian, because of the hypocrisy in the church and the confusion brought about by many different teachings coming from many different denominations and ministries.

That is when a good man visited me and told me that I needed to get into the Word of God for myself and find out the truth about all my questions and concerns. Since I had never done any serious research in my life to speak of, this seemed like an impossible task. I thought you had to go to Bible college to be trained to study the Bible, and I felt completely unqualified to try such a grand thing. Reluctantly, I went and bought a couple versions of the Bible, a concordance, a Greek dictionary, and a Hebrew dictionary. This was in late 1982. I began to study like my life depended on it. I eventually did exhaustive word studies on every topic I had been taught and eventually discovered that almost everything I had been taught in the churches was either totally false or only partly true, which makes it false. By the next year, I removed my family from the church world and taught them at home. As time went by, other people started meeting with us and I continued to study more and more about everything that came up concerning "Christianity" and the will of God.

Doors opened for me to speak about what I was learning from my studies. Over the next seven years, I spoke in prisons, different churches, various homes, seminars, Bible conferences, Christian men's meetings, and anywhere else I could. During this time, we still had a home church with a few families. All the while I owned and operated a transmission and auto repair shop. I never took any money from my speaking engagements or from the people I discipled. During the late eighties, I stopped traveling and began to focus more on my own family and marriage. As a result, I began to teach marriage seminars in my own city, since the family situation was so bad everywhere I went. Divorce in the church was very common and few men were leaders in their homes. Over the years, our home church grew bigger than our house or driveway could accommodate, so we started meeting in a rented space.

As of May 2018, I am seventy years of age. I have walked with God for thirty-eight-plus years. I have seriously studied the Scriptures for thirty-five-plus years of that time. I am very concerned about the American "Christian" church world. So many people are deceived. So many people don't seek God. So many people are in sin while they think they are going to heaven. So many people don't study the Scriptures, but just go by whatever the pastor tells them. So many pastors are just leading by repetition learned from traditions passed down to them, without taking any serious concern for the religious traditions they practice or for the souls and the lives of the people.

Therefore, so many people are going to hell and don't even know it. The purpose of this book and associated website is to try to stimulate people to seek God through study and prayer, so they might be a part of the very few who will be saved. The website, www. christianmyths.org, will eventually provide writings, audio and video teachings as well as links to worthwhile ministries as available. I hope that some people will wake up before it is too late. I hope you find the truth and have peace with God. Don't trust any man, not even me, but check out the Scriptures for yourself. There just can't be thousands of denominations with hundreds of ways to heaven with all being true at the same time. It is everyone's individual and personal responsibility to find the truth for themselves, and they cannot pay any man (pastor) to do that for them. Jesus said, "If *you* abide in my Word, then you would know the truth and the truth would set you free." May you abide in His word and know the truth and then you will be free and free indeed!

Sincerely,
Don Britton
Christianmyths.org@gmail.com
www.Christianmyths.org

Chapter 1

Traditions of Men/Christian Myths

The purpose of this book is to bring forth truth concerning the Bible and the many different myths people have about the Bible, God, salvation and the traditions they practice. It is amazing to me, that the vast majority of what the Bible teaches a Christian should be and do is not believed or practiced much today. On the other hand, the vast majority of what is taught, practiced in church and believed concerning God, Jesus, salvation and worship is not in the Bible. The fact that we have more than a thousand denominations today teaching a large variety of salvation plans, should give us great concern. In addition to that, there seems to be no limit to the different number of traditions and beliefs spread by these multiple thousands of denominations. Yet the Bible plainly teaches that there is only one gospel, one faith, one Lord and one way. Something has gone terribly wrong for it to be this way! The *traditions* of men and man-made *myths* have replaced the truth and have canceled out the Word of God!

We were warned by the Lord about this:

> *"See to it that no one takes you **captive** through philosophy and empty deception, according to the **tradition of men**, according to the elementary principles of the world, rather than according to Christ."*
> (Col. 2:8)

The prophet Isaiah saw this coming:

Then the Lord said, "Because this people draw near with their words And honor Me with their lip service, But they remove their hearts far from Me, And their reverence for Me consists of __tradition__ learned by __rote__." (Isa. 29:13)

Tradition learned by rote is the continual repetition of religious practices done week after week. No one seems to know exactly how they got started but after they are done for a while, they (the traditions) become the so-called "truth" and the Bible is no longer regarded as important for seeking the truth!

Here is what Jesus said about tradition:

And the Pharisees and the scribes asked Him, "Why do Your disciples not walk according to the tradition of the elders, but eat their bread with impure hands?" And He said to them, "Rightly did Isaiah prophesy of you hypocrites, as it is written, 'This people honors Me with their lips, But their heart is far away from Me. 'But in vain do they worship Me, Teaching as doctrines the precepts of men.' "Neglecting the commandment of God, you hold to the __tradition of men__." (Mar. 7:5–8)

More than one study has concluded that the modern American Christian church (all denominations included) has about the same morals as the secular society around it. The church members watch just about as much immoral and violent entertainment, including pornography. The church members are just about as willing to commit adultery and fornication. The church members worship the same idols of materialism, sports, ungodly entertainment and worldly pleasures as the rest of the world. Church members are about as involved in gossip, dishonesty, cheating, greed, love of money, anger, lust, immorality, un-forgiveness, jealously, and various chemical addictions as the rest of the world.

Unscriptural divorce is even more prevalent in the "church" than in the rest of the world. In fact, in day-to-day life, it has become very difficult, if not impossible to distinguish between a "so-called" believer and a non-believer by the way they act, talk and live since they are so similar. The church of today has no moral influence anymore on the world around it as it did in past decades, but the world now has tremendous influence on the church as well as the behavior and values of its members.

The norm now is that whatever the world is doing, the "church" is also doing. It appears that fewer than 2 percent (according to some studies) of all that claim to be a Christian have a serious relationship with God of fervent prayer, godliness, and serious study of the Scriptures. Most of our ministers today have no more of a relationship with God than the vast majority of their members do. They are mostly caught up in programs, building funds, meetings, and expanding their careers. The church of today has become a worldly social club led by mostly ungodly men who are experts at making people feel comfortable in their sins by tickling their ears with false teachings that are not found in the Bible and by practicing religious traditions created by men rather than God. These traditions are man-made myths and make people feel good (religious) but have nothing to do with righteousness and the will of God. The church of today, for the most part, has become part of the broad way that leads to hell! She has become a bride that is a harlot—unfaithful to her husband.

For the time will come when they will not endure sound doctrine; but wanting to have their ears tickled, they will accumulate for themselves teachers in accordance to their own desires; and will turn away their ears from the truth, and will turn aside to myths. (2 Tim. 4:3, 4)

Please read this book very carefully and seek out the truth for yourself. Your soul is at stake! You are only given one life here to determine if you are going to be a son or daughter of God forever! We must return to the Bible and adjust our theology to what the Scriptures say rather than what man has taught us because the traditions of men have replaced the Word of God!

> *Then the Lord said, "Because this people draw near with their words And honor Me with their lip service, But they remove their hearts far from Me, And their reverence for Me consists of tradition learned by rote."* (Isa. 29:13)

In other words, they go to the same place week after week, perform the same ceremonies over and over, participate in the same rituals time after time and do the same things over and over, again and again. They sing the same songs over and over, again and again.

They think that because they do these things they have served God and have pleased Him. They don't have a sincere, passionate, devoted, fervent, wholehearted relationship with God—just a form of religion that they do again and again outwardly, but it is not by the Spirit nor is it from the heart. It is just their tradition learned by rote (repetition) and it feels right to them. It is like the meaningless repetitions of the prayers of the Pharisees Jesus so hated.

> *But realize this, that in the last days difficult times will come. For men will be lovers of self, lovers of money, boastful, arrogant, revilers, disobedient to parents, ungrateful, <u>unholy</u>, unloving, irreconcilable, malicious gossips, without self-control, brutal, haters of good, treacherous, reckless, conceited, <u>lovers of pleasure rather than lovers of God</u>, **holding to a form of godliness**, although they have **denied its power**; Avoid such men as these.* (2 Tim. 3:1–5)

14

These are the last days and these men have a form of godliness (man-made religion), but they have no power to overcome sin, the world and the devil. They don't even know they have to or that they can. They are taught the lie that they can only be "practicing sinners saved by grace." Therefore, they have denied the power of God to overcome sin and live holy lives.

So consider what we have today; hundreds and hundreds of different kinds of "Christian" churches doing countless rituals and ceremonies each week, while the average "Christian" lives virtually no different than the rest of the world. Today's American church members engage in as much fleshly entertainment, un-forgiveness, adultery, fornication, gossip, greed, divorce, pornography, idolatry, etc., as the world around it does, not to mention the countless pastors who have had sex with their members, lied to the church about various issues and covered up sin practiced by other church leaders.

> *Therefore, prepare your minds for action, keep sober in spirit, fix your hope completely on the grace to be brought to you at the revelation of Jesus Christ. As obedient children, **do not be conformed to the former lusts** which were yours in your ignorance, but like the Holy One who called you, **be holy yourselves also in all your behavior;** because it is written, **"YOU SHALL BE HOLY, FOR I AM HOLY."** (1 Pet. 1:13–16)*

While all this hypocrisy is going on all the time they still gather everyone together each week and go through all the motions of so-called "worship" to God. All this sin in the church only proves that they honor God with their lips and in vain they worship Him. The rituals and ceremonies they practice are taught as doctrines and precepts of men, not because God asked for them, but because the pastors of today are more interested in pleasing the people than God. All God ever wanted was all their hearts with a sincere wholehearted relationship with Him, rather than their religion.

Today, the traditions and myths that come from them are the new standards. Whatever a church or denomination has done for a few years becomes the standard/tradition/myth and replaces the Scripture/Word of God after it is done or believed for a while.

For the purpose of this book, when I use the term "The Word of God," I will be referring to the Scriptures as found in the Bible. This is going to be the standard and reference I will use to back up everything written in this book. So please, study the Word of God for yourself and make sure that what I am saying is correct according to the Scriptures and not according to your religious views or the traditions you have had handed down to you.

> *Indeed, all who desire to live godly in Christ Jesus will be persecuted. But evil men and impostors will proceed from bad to worse, deceiving and being deceived. You, however, continue in the things you have learned and become convinced of, knowing from whom you have learned them, and that from childhood you have known the **sacred writings** which are able to give you the wisdom that leads to salvation through faith which is in Christ Jesus. **All Scripture** is inspired by God and profitable for **teaching**, for **reproof**, for **correction**, for **training in righteousness**; so that the man of God may be adequate, equipped for every good work.* (2 Tim. 3:12–17)

There are many denominations (thousands) today claiming to be Christian. There are also many ways given to be saved. It is not possible for all of them to be right at the same time. Something is very wrong with this whole system of "Christian religion." There can't be divisions among God's people and there can't be many different gospels and many different ways to heaven all at the same time. All of these different ways use the name of Jesus and all claim to have the way of life. This is impossible if you read the Bible and believe what it says. And in this book, I will attempt to document every statement with Scripture since all Scripture is inspired by God and is profitable for teaching and correction.

> *There is **one body** and **one Spirit**, just as also you were called in **one hope** of your calling; **one Lord, one faith, one baptism, one God** and **Father of all who is over all and through all and in all**.* (Eph. 4:4–6)

So if there is only one body (church) how do you know if you belong to the right one? They all say that they are the right one. If there is only one Spirit how can He be over the Baptist and the Catholic and the Presbyterian and the Pentecostal churches all at the same time? This very question should shake you up and wake you up to realize something is wrong, very, very wrong today.

You see, the Word of God just made it clear that there are not hundreds and hundreds of different kinds of churches that can be called Christian all at the same time nor is it possible to have many different gospels to go along with them all. There is only *ONE* church, only *ONE* gospel, only *ONE* faith and only *ONE* God.

This system of "Christianity" that we have today here in America has a different Jesus and a different "spirit" for each denomination and a different gospel and a different path to salvation for each one. Anyone who is honest with himself would have to admit that the Baptist spirit is different than the Catholic spirit, or that the Pentecostal spirit is not the same as the Lutheran spirit. You don't need a doctorate degree to see and understand that. So obviously, not everything that appears to be Christian is truly Christian. And since there is only one true church, where does that leave the vast majority of denominations today? And I am not suggesting that the true church is really one of the known denominations anyway. That will be cleared up more and more as read ahead.

So the reasonable question is this—is Christ divided up into thousands of denominations?

*Now I exhort you, brethren, by the name of our Lord Jesus Christ, **that you all agree** and that there be **no divisions among you**, but that you be made complete in the same mind and **in the same judgment**. For I have been informed concerning you, my brethren, by Chloe's people, that there are quarrels among you. Now I mean this, that each one of you is saying, "I am of Paul," and "I of Apollos," and "I of Cephas," and "I of Christ." **Has Christ been divided?** Paul was not crucified for you, was he? Or were you baptized in the name of Paul?* (1 Col. 1:10–13)

Does anyone really think that the many various denominations are in agreement on tradition, practice, doctrine or have the same judgment on biblical matters? So the question is, has Jesus Christ been divided into thousands of denominations with as many practices and traditions, not to mention the various doctrines and values they hold? Of course, Jesus is not divided, but is one with His father and one with the few who really know and serve Him. It is man who is divided up and man has created his own versions of Jesus. Man has created his own graven images of Jesus. The Baptists have a Baptist "jesus" and the Catholics have a Catholic "jesus" along with praying to mother Mary. The Pentecostals have a "mystical jesus" and the Faith Movement has a "prosperity jesus." None of these is the true Jesus who is an exact representation of His Father in heaven. Therefore, He is nothing like any of the denominational "jesuses" that each denomination has created for themselves.

*But I am afraid that, as the serpent deceived Eve by his craftiness, your minds will be led astray from the simplicity and purity of devotion to Christ. For if one comes and preaches **another Jesus whom we have not preached**, or you receive a **different spirit** which you have not received, or a **different*** *gospel which you have not accepted, you bear this beautifully.* (2 Col. 11:3–4)

The point is that the Scripture is no longer the standard used today for much of anything. As you read through chapter after chapter of this book, I hope you will see that more and more.

In this book, I will address a few of the most serious errors taught today as the traditions of men and explain why they are nothing more than man-made myths. Man-made myths that, in many cases, could cost you your soul!

As your read, I ask you to decide if the common belief that the church really can be divided up into many denominations and can practice any man-made tradition and believe anything they want is a *biblical truth or a myth*!

Chapter 2

The Myth of the Tithe

From the multitude of sermons on "tithing" you would get the impression that God had filled the Bible with hundreds of verses on paying the tithe to the church. But the fact is that there are fewer than twenty verses in the whole Bible that talk about the tithe and almost all of them are in the Old Testament and all of them are associated with the Old Testament Jewish law. It seems in some churches that a tithing message comes up every few Sundays as if that was one of the main things God had on His mind. Many Christians have been beaten down with this message and left to feel guilty if for some reason they could not come up with the 10 percent to put in the plate. It seems that many preachers stress that the tithe should be paid even before a past due mortgage or an unexpected medical expense. But what is the tithe? To whom was it to be paid? What was the purpose of the tithe? Does it have anything to do with the church today? Did any of the New Testament churches pay tithes? Did Paul instruct any of the churches to pay tithes? Let us find out if the modern teaching on tithing is a biblical *truth* or a *myth*?

I had to *pay the tithe*! That is what everybody always told me. I heard it from every "Christian" financial counselor I have ever talked with. And from every church I have ever been a part of in my thirty-eight-plus years of walking with God. I have heard a multitude of messages on tithing from many preachers. It sometimes seemed that a sermon on tithing would come up every time the building mortgage payment came due. I heard so much on tithing from ministers that I used to get the impression that God was more concerned with tithing than He was just about anything else. In fact, I used to have the impression that the subject of tithing was all over the Bible and that it was one of the main topics of the New Testament—that is, until I studied it out for myself!

So is tithing a requirement for a Christian who is led by the Holy Spirit in his giving or is it just another tradition handed down to us from the teachings of men?

> *And their reverence for Me consists of **tradition** learned by rote* (thoughtless repetition) (Isa. 29:13).

Tradition learned by rote is religious tradition learned by doing the same things again and again as you go through the same motions over and over again, week after week, without giving any serious thought as to why you are doing it. Why don't people ask why the pastor teaches law and grace at the same time? The tithe is of the law and grace is of Christ. Why do men who have a doctorate degree in Bible theology teach this? But week after week, virtually all the churches in America are tithing over and over again because of the traditions that have taken over and no one seems to notice.

So religious tradition does invalidate (render useless) the Word of God when it is practiced without correct biblical instruction as a basis for doing so. So is it biblical for the New Testament Church to preach and collect tithes or is it just another one of those myths most everyone believes without any regard for the Scriptures?

First of all, we need to find out what the tithe is and then why it was needed.

> *Thus all the tithe of the land, of the seed of the land or of the fruit of the tree, is the Lord's; it is holy to the Lord.* (Lev. 27:30)

"And to the sons of Levi (priesthood), *behold, I have given all the tithe in Israel for an inheritance, in return for their service which they perform, the service of the tent of meeting.* (Num. 18:21)

"For the tithe of the sons of Israel, which they offer as an offering to the Lord, I have given to the Levites for an inheritance; therefore, I have said concerning them, 'They shall have no inheritance (not allowed to own land) *among the sons of Israel.'"* (Num. 18:24)

"You shall surely tithe all the produce from what you sow, which comes out of the field every year." **(Deu. 14:22)**

So here it is obvious that the tithe was given to the Levitical priests who served in the tent of meeting and the temple. The Levites were not allowed to own land by which they could raise livestock and crops for food. Therefore, they were to eat from the tithe of the crops and livestock donated by everyone else. Take note of this fact—the tithe was *never* about money, it was always about *crops and livestock*. The main purpose was to *feed the Levites* because they had no land to produce their own food and it was also used to help widows and orphans.

But there was another way the tithe was to be used:

"And you shall eat (the tithe) *in the presence of the Lord your God, at the place where He chooses to establish His name, the tithe of your grain, your new wine, your oil, and the first-born of your herd and your flock, in order that you may learn to fear the Lord your God always. "And if the distance is so great for you that you are not able to bring the tithe, since the place where the Lord your God chooses to*

set His name is too far away from you when the Lord your God blesses you, then you <u>shall exchange it for money</u>, and bind the money in your hand and go to the place which the Lord your God chooses. "And you may <u>spend the money for whatever your heart desires, for oxen, or sheep, or wine, or strong drink, or whatever your heart desires</u>; and there <u>you shall eat</u> (the tithe) *in the presence of the Lord your God and <u>rejoice</u>, you and your household."*
(Deut. 14:23–26)

It is obvious that the tithe was not money since it had to be exchanged for money in order to make the trip. And since some preach the tithe as if it is for today, shouldn't they also tell you about this part—that you don't always have to bring your tithe to them, but sometimes you are supposed to eat and enjoy your tithe with your family?

I bet you never heard a sermon that you should take your own tithe and spend it on yourself and your family in order to rejoice before the Lord so that you would learn to fear the Lord your God, did you? You see, the Lord is the one who gives you everything and He can take it away as well! Do you wonder why your pastor never used this verse on tithing?

Did you know that there are 1,189 chapters in the Bible? Did you also know that out of those 1,189 chapters there are 31,173 verses containing about eight hundred thousand words? Consider this, out of the eight hundred thousand Hebrew and Greek words used, only thirty-five times do we find the words "tithe, tithes, or tithing" in the whole Bible and in fewer than twenty verses! That is not the impression most preachers leave about tithing and those thirty-five words are only found in sixteen locations in the Bible. In addition to that, only four of those locations are found in the New Testament and those four locations are in no way instructing us to pay tithes. Did you know that there is no record in the Bible of any New Testament church member ever paying tithes or being instructed to do so? So who started that tradition? It certainly wasn't Jesus or any of the apostles.

Did you know that there is no instruction written by any of the apostles to any of the churches to collect tithes or for any of the members to pay tithes?

Why would tithing be needed any longer since the Levitical priesthood was abolished with the death of Christ? Why would tithing be needed any longer since everyone is allowed to own land and provide his own food? And since Jesus abolished the priesthood and temple worship, He also eliminated the need for the storehouse to keep the crops and livestock that would be eaten by the Levitical priest and given to the widows and orphans. So is it any wonder that no one in the New Testament collected tithes, paid tithes or taught anyone to do either? So why do so many churches teach that we have to pay tithes today? Could it be that the traditions and teachings of men have invalidated the Word of God just as the Scriptures said? Could it be that this teaching is self-serving to many preachers to fulfill their own goals, including securing their own income and funding the many programs they want or maybe to build a big and expensive building to bring glory to themselves?

Do you wonder why most all tithe teachers of today use these verses to teach about the tithe, while leaving out the other ones listed above?

> *"Will a man rob God? Yet you are robbing Me! But you say, 'How have we robbed you?' In tithes and offerings.* "You are cursed with a curse, for you are robbing Me, the whole nation of you! *"Bring the whole tithe into the storehouse, so that there may be food* (something to eat) *in My house* (for the temple priest)*, and test Me now in this,"* says the Lord of hosts, *"if I will not open for you the windows of heaven, and pour out for you a blessing until it overflows."* (Mal. 3:8–10)

The storehouse was in the temple building and the tithe was kept there to feed the Levites who served there, so what does that have to do with the church today? Why do ministers still preach law and grace at the same time? Isn't it really about the money? Money for programs, buildings, and preachers? And since the tithe never was about money to begin with and since the priesthood has been abolished and the storehouse is no longer used, why would any modern preacher teach a Christian believer that he had to tithe, that is if he used the Bible to teach from? Remember, the tithe was *never about money*, but was always about food for the priest and the needy.

But are we to give? Of course, we are, but not according to the letter of the law. Let each man be led by the Spirit and give as he has purposed in his own heart.

> *Let each one do just as he has purposed in his heart;*
> *not grudgingly or under compulsion; for God loves a*
> *cheerful giver.* (2 Col. 9:7)

You see, this is a heart thing, not a law thing.

> *For all who are being led by the Spirit of God, these*
> *are sons of God.* (Rom. 8:14)

If you are being led by the Spirit, you are not under the law.

So giving is a heart thing directed by the Holy Spirit and tithing is of the law for the purposes we have already revealed.

> *For as many as are of the __works of the Law are__*
> *__under a curse__; for it is written, "Cursed is every-*
> *one who does not abide by all things written in the*
> *book of the law, to perform them." Now that __no one__*
> *is justified by the Law before God is evident; for,*
> *"The righteous man shall live by faith." However,*
> *the __Law is not of faith__; on the contrary, "He who*
> *practices them shall live by them.* (Gal. 3:10–12)

So why would you tithe according to the law since it is not of faith but only legalism practiced by rote? And then why would you not give according to leading of the Holy Spirit by faith? Who did Jesus and the apostles teach us to give to anyway? Was it not the poor and the brothers and sisters in the body of Christ who were in need? We were never taught to give to preachers anywhere. We should give to anyone the Holy Spirit leads us to, but not according to a law imposed upon us by preachers!

We should also give to the true church. The church does need some money for the cost in promoting the gospel as well as a simple meeting place and the few expenses that go with that and also to help the poor. The true church does not need to have a paid staff, but only sincere volunteers. There were no paid ministers or paid staff members in the New Testament church. So the money collected then was used for helping those in need like the widows, the poor and the orphans, but not for paying preachers.

Obviously, the modern teachings on tithing are nothing more than falsehood. They are teachings of men that have been handed down to us for the purposes of men. This tradition has robbed many widows and poor people by extorting money from them, that often they could not afford to pay, by preachers who falsely teach that they must obey the law or they will be cursed. Sadly, many dear souls who struggle to make a mortgage payment and feed their children are under the same false impression that they must give 10 percent of what they earn to the church, so the preachers could be paid and build fancy buildings for their own glory. This false teaching has resulted in many feeling guilty and coming under condemnation for feeding their children and paying for their home first, when they did not have enough left over to pay the 10 percent to the church. This is outrageous and a great lie!

Jesus would never rob or pressure the poor nor did any of the Apostles make them feel guilty about not being able to pay a tithe. The Apostles never even mentioned the tithe.

> *"Woe to you, scribes and Pharisees, hypocrites, because **you devour widows' houses**, even while for a pretense you make long prayers; therefore, you shall receive greater condemnation."* (Matt. 23:14)

How many widows and poor people have been robbed by the tithe teaching? Have you ever wondered if the preaching of the tithe has anything to do with preachers being paid? That raises another question. Are preachers supposed to be paid? Is it biblical to pay preachers? The answer is in the next chapter.

This is what Paul the apostle did for his income:

> *For you yourselves know how you ought to **follow our example**, because we did not act in an undisciplined manner among you, nor did we eat anyone's bread without paying for it, but with **labor and hardship** we kept **working night and day** (making tents) **so that we might not be a burden to any of you; not because we do not have the right to this** (to eat food), but in order to offer ourselves as a model for you, that you might **follow our example**. For even when we were with you, we used to give you this order: if **anyone** (anyone includes preachers) will not work, **neither let him eat.** (2 Thess. 3:7–10)

The right Paul referred to was to *eat food*, not collect money from anyone for himself. And Paul certainly did not pass a collection plate and collect tithes from anyone! If the principle of "will not work, neither let him eat" was followed today there would be a lot of hungry preachers.

So how would you judge the modern teaching on tithing, is it a biblical *truth* or a *myth*?

Chapter 3

The Myth of the Paid Pastor

The question is not how much should a preacher be paid, but if he should be paid at all for doing what God has gifted and called him to do? There are a variety of gifts and ministries given to the church by the Holy Spirit for the common good of the Body. Why should only the pastor's gift and a few "staff" members be paid for their gifts when all the others serve on a voluntary basis? Who decided that? Why are the pastors at the top of the list of those getting salaries? Didn't the apostles and Jesus teach that we should not show partiality and that even the less seemly members be given more abundant honor so that all members would be recognized as necessary? Didn't Jesus say that the greatest among you would be the servant of all, not the highest paid of all? Why are there no righteous men in the Bible who were paid for their service to God and His people?

Not only did they not receive pay, but they actually refused to take anything from the people they brought the Word of God to. Righteous men clearly understand that when you are paid by the very people you are to bring the Word of God to, that the money will eventually affect the message and the messenger will end up pleasing the people rather than God. Isn't that what we have today, paid preachers who give smooth, ear-tickling messages that keep everyone comfortable in their sins? Where is the preacher who is free from the approval of man and the love of sordid gain? Where is the preacher who will confront the sinner in the church and call the members to repentance? Read on and see if the idea that a preacher should be paid is a biblical *truth* or *myth*!

In the nineties, I once had a discussion with one of my vendors at my business. He told me that his pastor made six figures at his church, plus various other financial benefits including an expense account, clothing expenses, insurance, retirement, and an occasional love offering for vacation, etc. I said that he must really preach a lot for that kind of money. He said, "Oh yes, he preaches for about thirty minutes on Sunday morning, about thirty minutes on Sunday night and about thirty minutes on Wednesday night."

I said, "Wow, so he only preaches one and a half hours per week for all that money?"

He said, "Well, he does more than that."

I said, "Like what?"

He said, "Well, he prays and studies his Bible."

I said, "So you pay him for that. Shouldn't everyone do that?"

He said, "Well, he does more than that."

I said, "Like what?"

He said, "Like, visits the sick in the hospital."

So I responded to him this way: "So let me get this straight, you pay him $100,000 plus benefits per year to preach an hour and a half per week, study his Bible for you and pray for you and visit your sick friends in the hospital?"

I told him that I preached a lot more than that for free, studied my own Bible and did my own praying and when one of my friends got sick, I visited them myself. And doing all that while I worked fifty to sixty hours per week in my business. I told him he could not hire someone to take away his responsibility to know God, to know his Word, to pray to God and visit the sick for himself. He was very offended. Have you ever thought about this type of thing? Does it make any sense to you? Have you studied the Bible to see what it says for yourself?

There is no case in the Bible of any righteous man of God ever making a vocation (job for pay) out of preaching the Word of God.

Notice what Jesus told his disciples concerning getting paid when they preached:

> *"And as you go, **preach**, saying, 'The kingdom of heaven is at hand.' "Heal the sick, raise the dead, cleanse the lepers, cast out demons; **freely you received, freely give.** "Do not acquire gold, or silver, or copper for your money belts, or a bag for your journey, or even two tunics, or sandals, or a staff; for the **worker is worthy of his support.**
> (Matt. 10:7–10)

Notice that the first thing Jesus told them was "freely you received, freely give." That clearly means the gospel did not cost them anything and they could not charge for preaching it! Who changed that?

The second thing Jesus told them was "do not acquire (get or take) gold, silver or copper for your money belts." In other words, these men with mission assignments were not to take any money along with them. Jesus told them they would have their necessities provided for. Having necessities provided for while on a mission trip is a long way from charging for the gospel or preaching as a pastor for pay at home.

The third thing Jesus said was that the worker was worthy of his support. This seems strange after saying "freely you received, freely give," until we study a little further. The Greek word used here for support is *trophe*, which means physical nourishment for the body, as in getting to eat food. These apostles were allowed to eat food when traveling away from their homes to preach. So food, shelter, etc., was their *support*, not money! Apparently, the reason they were allowed to eat food away from home was because they were away from their normal ability to provide food for themselves as they usually did. Why don't men who study the Bible and who went to Bible school or seminary tell us this?

Jesus also told his disciples this when he sent them out to preach—

> *"Go your ways; behold, I send you out as lambs in the midst of wolves. "Carry no purse, no bag, no shoes; and greet no one on the way. "And whatever house you enter, first say, 'Peace be to this house.' "And if a man of peace is there, your peace will rest upon him; but if not, it will return to you. "__And stay in that house, eating and drinking what they give you; for the laborer is worthy of his wages.__ Do not keep moving from house to house. "And whatever city you enter, and they receive you, __eat what is set before you.__* (Luke 10:3–8)

Again, the wages for preaching, if you *travel away from home*, is only food and shelter and certainly any personal necessities one might have while on the trip. The wages here are not what we would normally associate as wages today and certainly are NOT MONEY!

So again, Jesus clearly tells them to carry no purse. You see they did not need a purse if they were not going to collect any money. Nor did they need a purse to pay for food and lodging if they were going to stay in somebody's house with all necessities provided for. Also, Jesus again made it clear that their wages were food, drink, and lodging, etc. Again, no money was associated with these "wages" or "support," only basic necessities. In fact, they were forbidden to receive money for doing what God called them to do!

So do you see how traditions handed down to us from the past have invalidated the Word of God and made it to no effect? What preacher have you ever heard preach these scriptures explaining that the support and wages for the preacher were not money, but only for the traveling preacher who was allowed to stay and eat at someone's home and was not allowed to collect any money? So it is obvious that the preacher/pastor can't take money for doing the work of God.

In 2 Kings 5, Elisha the prophet of God refused to receive money from Naaman after he was healed of leprosy. But Elisha's servant Gehazi took two talents of silver and two changes of clothes from Naaman without Elisha's knowledge. When Elisha discovered what Gehazi had done he said:

> *Then he said to him, "Did not my heart go with you, when the man turned from his chariot to meet you? Is it a time to receive money and to receive clothes and olive groves and vineyards and sheep and oxen and male and female servants* (for doing the work of God)*? "Therefore, the leprosy of Naaman shall cleave to you and to your descendants forever." So he went out from his presence a leper as white as snow.*
> (2 Kings 5:26–27)

So Gehazi was cursed for accepting money and other benefits for the work of God done through Elisha. Wasn't the gift of God freely received and shouldn't it be freely given? Elisha made it clear that it was not acceptable to receive material gifts or financial compensation of any kind for doing what God had called him to do.

Another point here is that the church is not to be governed by a single pastor. The church is supposed to be governed by a body of elders. They are often called overseers. Notice that Paul always appointed elders (plural), not a pastor (singular) to manage the new church. The idea of one man leading the church probably came from the "pope" mentality of the Catholic Church and stayed with the protestant movement making the pastor the head of the church. These elders should function in their different gifts as apostles, pastors, evangelist, prophets and teachers. Jesus never intended that one man could exercise all the gifts necessary for the building up of the body until it becomes mature, to the measure and stature that belongs to Christ. This probably won't happen unless all the equipping gifts are working. And none of these gifted men should be paid for this.

This is not a vocation, but a gift and duty. Congregations should not be very large and should have multiple elders/overseers to equipment the saints. If the overseers work for a living and teach and equip the saints in their time off from work, the church would be much better off. Today, we have a church system with one pastor managing programs, entertainment, staff, finances, building maintenance, construction, budgets, marketing, weddings, funerals, and very often hundreds if not thousands of members. This is not the discipling and equipping of the saints Jesus intended. One elder can only disciple a few families. Several elders can disciple several families. What if the elders left the large church situation and organized home churches with one or two leaders that worked for a living and discipled small numbers of members in their homes. It would all be free, no salaries, no construction, no budgets, no marketing, no staff, and no one being left out of being discipled!

Even if a larger group had to rent some meeting space, this would be fairly inexpensive compared to paying pastors and staff members. During the last thirty-seven years, I have discipled many couples and individuals without pay. All the while, I owned and operated an auto repair business full time. I also raised a family and spent a lot of time studying the Word of God. You see, anyone can find time for what they love to do. Some men love hunting or football or camping or fishing and spend a lot of time and money on these things while working a fulltime job. What if a man loved God and wanted to make a difference for the Kingdom of God? Couldn't he find time after working for a living, to serve the Lord and do it without any compromise of the truth?

After all, there are 168 hours in a week. If forty hours were spent working for a living, and fifty-six hours spent sleeping, that still leaves seventy-two hours to do something with. This is the time we choose what we do with. Of course, some is for family time and some for our marriage and some for personal use, but still we could salvage maybe one fourth of the seventy-two hours and maybe use eighteen hours a week for study, teaching, discipling and building up the kingdom of God. I dare say that very few paid pastors invest that much time in actually building the Kingdom of God each week, because they are so caught up in church "business," religious programs, building programs, marketing programs, budgets, planning ceremonies, directing staff, going to speaking engagements of no real importance to God, boosting their ministry, counseling unrepentant members, doing little or no real work at all and living the life of the "clergy," looking for the respectful greetings in the "marketplaces" and the chief seats in the "temples." So a godly man, could easily work for a living, and do lots of worthwhile work for the kingdom of God without being paid as a pastor.

> *And He gave some as apostles, and some as prophets, and some as evangelists, and some as pastors and teachers, **for the equipping of the saints for the work of service**, to the building up of the body of Christ; **until we all attain to the unity of the faith**, and of the knowledge of the Son of God, to a mature man, to the measure of the stature which belongs to the fullness of Christ. **As a result, we are no longer to be children**, tossed here and there by waves and **carried about by every wind of doctrine, by the trickery of men**, by craftiness in deceitful scheming; but speaking the truth in love, we are to grow up in all aspects into Him who is the head, even Christ, from whom the whole body, being fitted and held together by what every joint supplies, according to the proper working of each individual part, causes the growth of the body for the building up of itself in love.* (Eph. 4:11–16)

In Numbers chapter 16, Moses a servant of God had to deal with the rebellion of Korah. Korah and several men rose up against

Moses and his leadership and rebelled against him. When Moses cried out to God he said,

> *Then Moses became very angry and said to the Lord, "Do not regard their offering! I have* **not taken a single donkey from them**, *nor have I done harm to any of them."* (Num. 16:15)

As minister and leader of God's people, Moses could say with confidence that he had taken nothing from any of the people, not even a donkey. Therefore, Moses had not been tempted to please the people, but was free to say only what God was saying and some did not like it and rebelled against him. It is very hard, no, virtually impossible for men to take money and gifts from their members and still please God, because they will end up pleasing the people instead. When men are paid to preach it is very difficult if not impossible for them to be objective and preach only what God says especially if the people *don't like it*! Moses stayed clear of any temptation to compromise what God was saying to the people by never taking *anything* from them. How rare it is today to find this kind of integrity in a minister. To refuse to take anything from the people and to serve the people and God because it is in his heart, not because he makes a living doing it. This should be a lesson for us today.

The faithful prophet of God, Samuel, had this to say about being paid:

> *"And now, here is the king walking before you, but I am old and gray, and behold my sons are with you. And I have walked before you* **from my youth even to this day.** *"Here I am; bear witness against me before the Lord and His anointed.* **Whose ox have I taken**, *or* **whose donkey have I taken**, *or* **whom have I defrauded? Whom have I oppressed, or from whose hand have I taken a bribe to blind my eyes with it?** *I will restore it to you." And they*

*said, "**You have not defrauded us**, or **oppressed us**, or **taken anything from any man's hand**." And he said to them, "The Lord is witness against you, and His anointed is witness this day that **you have found nothing in my hand**." And they said, "He is witness."* (1 Sam. 12:2–5)

So Samuel spent his whole life as a preacher of the Word of God in Israel and never took anything from any man. Not a single gift or offering or benefit at all. Samuel indicated that if he had taken anything, then he would have received a bribe and it would have blinded his eyes. I wonder how many men down through the ages have had their eyes blinded by taking money and gifts to preach. There is no doubt that this compromise is the standard for today.

Here is how it works. The preacher/pastor receives money and gifts from the ones he is supposed to be instructing in right living, correcting those who do wrong, rebuking those who continue to do wrong and removing those from the church who won't repent. But having taken the money and gifts from the very people he is supposed to be holding to an account for their sins, he will be blinded from seeing their sins or confronting them. So in order to keep his customers (church members) happy and keep them coming back and the money flowing, he will go easy on them or altogether eliminate correcting and rebuking sinful behavior. Therefore, his messages will be more ear tickling in nature and he will say things like *"we are all just sinners saved by grace"* or *"we are just going to love everybody here"* or *"it is not the personality of this church to correct people,"* in order to excuse the sins of the people. He will teach the popular false doctrines of the day which "allow" people to feel comfortable in their sins, causing them to believe that they are going to heaven while they live in a carnal lifestyle. And since his eyes are blinded by the bribe of receiving money and gifts from the very people he is supposed to be guiding away from living in sin, he now accepts the sins of the people as a normal part of being a Christian. And since he himself is *blind* to the dangers of sin, he will lead the people to the pit of hell along with himself.

> *And He also spoke a parable to them:* "__*A blind man cannot guide a blind man,*__ *can he?* __*Will they not both fall into a pit?*__" (Luke 6:39)

I wonder how many millions of people are in hell right now because they listened to a paid preacher tell them that they were alright with God. This is certainly still going on now, because the church in America today is full of people practicing sin. It is clear in the Bible that if you willfully commit sin that you are on the way to destruction. And what funeral did you ever go to that the paid preacher didn't preach the deceased person right on into heaven, even though everybody knew how he or she really lived here on the earth? You see, this practice itself gives people a false hope and a false sense of security.

Speaking of false teachers Jude had this to say:

> *Woe to them! For they have gone the way of Cain, and* __*for pay*__ *they have rushed headlong into the* __*error of Balaam*__*, and perished in the rebellion of Korah.* (Jud. 1:11)

If you study Balaam, he was a man who knew God, but was willing to compromise and prophesy against the children of Israel for the money he was paid. The money blinded his eyes and he was willing to make compromises because of it. In other words, he preached and said what the people who paid him wanted him to say. Again, this is a warning for the present time!

Paul the apostle said this:

> *For it is written in the Law of Moses, "You shall not muzzle the ox while he is threshing." God is not concerned about oxen, is He? Or is He speaking*

*altogether for our sake? **Yes, for our sake** (preach-ers) it was written, because the plowman ought to plow in hope, and the thresher to thresh in hope of **sharing the crops**. If we **sowed spiritual things** in you, is it too much if we should **reap material things from you?** If others share the right over you, do we not more? Nevertheless, we **did not use** this right, but we endure all things, that we may cause no hindrance to the gospel of Christ. Do you not know that those who perform sacred services **eat the food of the temple**, and those who attend regularly to the altar have **their share with the altar**? So also, the Lord directed those who pro-claim the gospel to **get their living from the gospel**.* (1 Col. 9:9–14)

So Paul made it clear that according to the law that he, as a minister, had a right to receive material things when he had sown spiritual things. Again, he wasn't talking about a salary, love offerings, or other valuable assets, but simply about *food*. Just like those who were able to eat the food at the temple. This was the living he was referring to; food, drink and shelter. But notice that Paul did not use his right to *EAT* other people's food without paying for it. He said that he did not want to cause any hindrance to the gospel of Christ. Could it be the concern for the bribe principle, blinding one's eyes from being straightforward to the ones from whom you are receiving food? Where is the preacher like this today? Most preachers I know, not only want to be paid, but expect others to pay for their meals when they go out to dinner.

What makes a preacher think he should be treated in a special way? The word "clergy" is not in the Bible. Why should a preacher be paid or have his own special parking place? Isn't this kind of treat-ment reserved for kings and princes of the world? Didn't Jesus say that the greatest among you would be the servant of all?

Again, notice what else Paul had to say about this:

> *Now we command you, brethren, in the name of our Lord Jesus Christ, that you keep aloof from every brother who leads an* **unruly life** *and not according to the tradition which you received from us. For you yourselves know how you ought to* **follow our example**, *because we did not act in an undisciplined manner among you,* **nor did we eat anyone's bread without paying for it**, *but with labor and hardship we kept working night and day so that we might* **not be a burden to any of you; not because we do not have the right to this**, *but in order* **to offer ourselves as a model for you**, *that you might* **follow our example**. *For even when we were with you, we used to give you this order: if anyone* (including preachers) *will not work, neither let him eat.* (2 Thess. 3:6–10)

Paul was a preacher and a tent maker. Paul did not consider preaching to be a vocation. No one in the Bible had a vocation of preaching. Paul's vocation was making tents. He had freely received the gospel from the Lord, and for free, Paul preached it. Even though Paul had a right to eat food as a minister of the gospel, he did not exercise that right. This right never was about taking money or being paid as a preacher, but only about whether or not he would eat someone else's food. In fact, Paul did not eat without paying for his food and he admonished all ministers to follow his example in this. This is New Testament instruction! Again, see how far we have drifted from the will of God and from what the Scriptures teach!

> Jesus said in John 10:1–2, 8–12 *"Truly, truly, I say to you,* **he who does not enter by the door** *into the fold of the sheep, but climbs up some other way,* **he is a thief and a robber**. *"But he*

who enters by the door is a __shepherd of the sheep__. "All (pastors/shepherds) *who came before Me __are thieves and robbers__, but the sheep did not hear them. "__I am the door__; if anyone enters through Me, he shall be saved, and shall go in and out, and find pasture. "__The thief comes only to steal, and kill, and destroy__; I came that they might have life, and might have it abundantly. "__I am the good shepherd__; the good shepherd lays down His life for the sheep. "__He who is a hireling, and not a shepherd__, who is not the owner of the sheep, beholds the wolf coming, and leaves the sheep, and flees, and the wolf snatches them, and scatters them. "__He flees because he is a hireling and is not concerned about the sheep__."*

Here Jesus said, that the shepherd (pastor) who is financially compensated for his duties as a pastor is a *hireling*, and that a hireling, a paid pastor, is not the shepherd of God's sheep. I know this is a hard statement, so what are you going to do with it? Can you accept what Jesus said? He didn't give any exceptions to this, so can you?

The thief who came to steal, kill and destroy in this passage is not Satan as most pastors have taught, but is the paid (hireling) pastor himself! The topic here is about shepherds (pastors), not Satan. A pastor who comes into the fold of the sheep by some other way (being paid), other than the door (Jesus) by taking money for preaching, is a thief and a robber. This paid pastor is not like Paul, Elisha, Samuel, Moses, John, Peter, or any other righteous man of God. This pastor loves sordid gain (money he did not work for). These pastors rob members of their money to pay themselves and in the process, steal their souls because they tickle ears and compromise the Word of God. These shepherds leave out the judgments and warnings of God and preach "easy believism," "false grace" and give a false hope of salvation to the many. These paid pastors teach some form of eternal security to people who still live in sin. Every time someone dies, the hireling "preaches" them to heaven, tickling the ears of everyone at the funeral.

Also, these hirelings don't teach about the narrow way and how few enter eternal life. They also leave out repentance, one's personal cross and self-denial of sin and worldliness which is required for salvation. The hireling leaves the impression that virtually everyone in church goes to heaven, and many outside church, even though Jesus plainly taught that only a few will enter life. They pervert grace and make it into a license to sin. The reason they do this is *because* they are hirelings. Hirelings are paid preachers blinded by bribes (financial gain) and the traditions of men. Hirelings are the ones who continually preach about tithing, even though they should know that tithing never was about money and has nothing to do with the church. They preach tithing because it is the source of their income. Hirelings are not the shepherds of God. If you can be hired, you can be fired! Who could have ever fired Paul, Peter, Jesus, Samuel, Moses, or any other man of God? It is the hireling, the paid shepherd (pastor) that came to steal, kill and destroy! He will steal your money, family, time and your soul by leaving out the warnings of God and the sense of urgency while keeping you busy with religious activity.

> *Therefore, I exhort the elders among you, as your fellow elder and witness of the sufferings of Christ, and a partaker also of the glory that is to be revealed, shepherd the flock of God among you, exercising oversight not under compulsion, but **voluntarily**, according to the will of God; and not for **sordid gain**, but with eagerness; nor yet as lording it over those allotted to your charge, but proving to be examples to the flock. And when the Chief Shepherd appears, you will receive the unfading crown of glory.* (1 Pet. 5:1–4)

Here, Peter plainly says for the shepherd (pastor) to serve *voluntarily* according to the will of God (which is without pay) and not for sordid gain (taking money others have worked for). If he shepherds in this way (without pay), only then will he receive his crown of glory when Jesus comes. So where does that leave the hireling when Jesus comes?

Unjust/sordid gain: To gain or profit from the assets or work of others, to take money you did not earn, to gain from stealing, extortion or deception. It is also called filthy lucre, dirty money, and dishonest gain. When preachers teach and preach the tithe, they are preaching a lie and personally gain from the deception of it. As a result, they manipulate the hearer into giving at least ten percent by putting him under the pressure that he has to give according to the letter of the law or he could be cursed. Even if the member is struggling financially he is pressured to give the required 10 percent tithe anyway. Some churches now have credit card terminals in the pews. The push is always for money, money and more money. This is nothing more than extortion by the pastors and is very evil. Many widows and poor people have been devastated by this. Television preachers promise wealth and healing if only you will send them your money. And when any pastor brings in a special speaker, he again pressures the members to give big so his preacher buddy will gain a big profit off the member's hard earned money.

And have you ever noticed if there is an ungodly member who is a "big tither," how the pastor will chum up to him and never address his sin? And the pastor always has time and attention for anything the "big tither" wants. But if some poor person needs help from the pastor, he or she has to make an appointment and gets little attention. It is like this:

> *For if a man comes into your assembly with a gold ring and dressed in fine clothes, and there also comes in a poor man in dirty clothes, and you pay special attention to the one who is wearing the fine clothes, and say, "You sit here in a good place," and you say to the poor man, "You stand over there, or sit down by my footstool," have you not made distinc-*

tions among yourselves, and become judges with evil motives? (Jas. 2:2–4)

The scriptures plainly tell us that a leader/overseer/shepherd/pastor/minister, is to not be given over to sordid/unjust gain because it blinds their eyes.

*His watchmen are **blind**, All of them know nothing. **All of them** are mute dogs unable to bark* (barking is for warning)*, Dreamers lying down, who love to slumber; And the dogs are greedy, they are not satisfied. And **they are shepherds who have no understanding**; They have all turned to their own way, Each one to his **unjust gain**, **to the last one**.* (Isa. 56:10–11)

Pastors are supposed to be watchmen warning the people of dangers to their souls, but when they are willing to take the unjust gain from the people, they become blind and then tickle ears to please the people (their source of money) rather than please God by telling the people what God really wants them to hear. And since most people want their ears tickled, the paid pastors are more than willing to do it for the money and the position they want.

*For the overseer must be above reproach as God's steward, not self-willed, not quick-tempered, not addicted to wine, not pugnacious, not fond of **sordid gain**—* (Tit. 1:7)

Here are some examples of preachers who have been excessive in taking sordid (unjust) gain. Take note of the net worth (as found on the web) of some well-known preachers who have spent their lives teaching and preaching tithing, rapture, false grace and eternal security. According to information found on the internet, Charles Stanley—1.5 million. He also is paid an undisclosed amount by First

Baptist of Atlanta and also receives $299,000 per year from In-Touch Ministries. John Macarthur, earns nearly 1 million per year with his net worth in the millions; John Hagee, 5 million; Joel Osteen, 40 million; Joyce Meyers, 8 million; Benny Hinn, 42 million; Billy Graham, 25 million; Creflo Dollar, 27 million; TD Jakes, 18 million; Pat Robinson, 100 million; Jerry Falwell Jr., 10 million; Kenneth Copeland, hundreds of Millions. Besides these preachers, there are hundreds of thousands of pastors, evangelists and Bible teachers with various salaries and paid benefits for preaching and teaching what was freely given to them and the American church is no better off with most all of them, since the church is so mired down in sin and worldliness like never before.

How could it be possible that all these preachers took for themselves all that money from donations given to their ministries intended for promoting the gospel without being guilty of taking sordid/unjust gain and blinding their own eyes? Wasn't one of the qualifications for being an overseer of the church, to be free from the love of money? These are not the shepherds of God, but hirelings. No humble servant of God could ever take such huge amounts of money for himself! Not to mention the many hirelings who just take nice salaries with benefits each week. Jesus said that the hireling that preaches the gospel for pay is a thief and a robber who comes only to steal, kill and destroy souls since he is a wolf in sheep's clothing. Also, you should be concerned at how well these men are spoken of by most everyone. Men who preach the true Words of God are always persecuted and slandered just like Jesus, Paul, Moses, Elijah, Jeremiah, Peter, and all the messengers of God were in the old days according to the Scriptures. Why do we think it should be any different now?

"Woe to you when __all men speak well of you__, for their fathers used to treat the __false prophets__ in the same way." (Luke 6:26)

Look at how popular some men are, like Charles Stanley or Billy Graham or John Macarthur or Benny Hinn or T. D. Jakes or Rick Warren just to name a few. They are not hated like Jesus or the apostles were, not to mention all the prophets that were killed bringing the Word of God to a rebellious nation, Israel. Don't we have a rebellious nation now and a modern church that is full of sin and worldliness today? Then why are these men so popular if they are really saying what God is saying to a church full of sin and to a rebellious nation as we are? These men are not only very popular, but they have completely failed to address the condition of the church and to call the masses that follow them to repentance, yet they have made millions from the unsuspecting givers without giving them the slightest lasting benefit and no one seems to notice that they are wolves in sheep's clothing.

"The anger of the LORD will not turn back Until He has performed and carried out the purposes of His heart; In the last days you will clearly understand it. "I did not send these prophets, But they ran. I did not speak to them, But they prophesied. "But if they had stood in My council, Then they would have announced My words to My people, And would have turned them back from their evil way And from the evil of their deeds. "I have heard what the prophets have said who prophesy falsely in My name, saying, 'I had a dream, I had a dream!' "How long? Is there anything in the hearts of the prophets who prophesy falsehood, even these prophets of the deception of their own heart, who intend to make My people forget My name by their dreams which they relate to one another, just as their fathers forgot My name because of Baal? "The prophet who has a dream may relate his dream, but let him who has My word speak My word in truth. What does straw have in common with grain?" declares the

> LORD. *"**Is not My word like fire?**" declares the
> LORD, "**and like a hammer which shatters a
> rock?** "Therefore behold, I am against the proph-
> ets," declares the LORD, "who steal My words from
> each other. "Behold, I am against the prophets,"
> declares the LORD, "who use their tongues and
> declare, 'The Lord declares.' "Behold, I am against
> those who have prophesied false dreams," declares
> the LORD, "and related them and led My people
> astray by their falsehoods and reckless boasting; yet I
> did not send them or command them, **nor do they
> furnish this people the slightest benefit**," declares
> the LORD.* (Jer. 23:20–22, 25–32)

Today's popular prophets, pastors and evangelists are not bringing the Word of God that is like fire and a hammer, but a soft, easy
word of false grace, false mercy and false love. They leave out the
truth about God's judgment and wrath on disobedient sons. They
teach salvation by "sinners prayer," rather than teach that repentance
from sin and bearing fruit and enduring faithful until the end is necessary for eternal life. Today's popular preachers have made the very
narrow way that leads to life, quite wide instead, so that it appears
that virtually everybody can enter in. The gospel has been perverted
by today's preachers for sordid gain and the approval of men.

Man-made religion has become a multi-billion dollar industry
and in all this the morals of our nation and the church have gone
down, down, down. Let every preacher get a job or start a business,
earn his own income and make disciples of Jesus, rather than false
converts. If he can't volunteer to do this from his heart, then he is not
fit for service to God!

Notice what Jesus did concerning the merchandising of the
things of God:

> *Then they *came to Jerusalem. And He entered
> the temple and began to drive out those who were*

__buying and selling__ in the temple, and overturned the tables of the __money changers__ and the seats of those __who were selling__ doves; and He would not permit anyone to carry __merchandise__ through the temple. And He began to teach and say to them, "Is it not written, 'MY HOUSE SHALL BE CALLED A HOUSE OF PRAYER FOR ALL THE NATIONS'? But you have __made it a ROBBERS' DEN__." (Mar. 11:15–17)

We now know that the true temple is the church, the people of God, not a physical building, and that this house of God, the people (the true church), is not to have any buying and selling going on in it (the church). No one is to merchandise the things of God nor the gospel of God. No money should be exchanging hands for the things of God. Freely we received and freely we give. Today we have religious merchandise branded under the name of "Christian" that has become a multibillion dollar industry with countless ministries taking in billions of dollars with countless ministers, staff members, pastors, evangelists, Bible teachers, Bible schools, counselors, Bible professors, etc., receiving pay for having a vocation in the things of God. And they are merchandising countless books, CDs, videos, Bible courses, prayer cloths, holy water, music, anointing oil, promises of healing, promises of wealth, promises of salvation, tickling of ears and whatever else the people want to hear, for the profit of money. Oh, how Jesus will turn over their money tables in judgment. Oh, the judgment on those who have lived the soft, easy lifestyle of the paid minister. These are the ones who are hirelings, who don't shepherd for Jesus, but for money, reputation and the approval of man. Woe be to them for their judgment will be forever.

I once belonged to a fairly large church where the pastor had control of the budget. At some point, I got a copy of the budget and discovered that the "senior" pastor paid himself well over six figures per year, various other financial benefits plus bonuses and retirement contributions. What was shocking was that the associate pastor, who was a very hard worker, only got paid about fifteen thousand per year. The associate pastor had a wife and two kids and drove an old Dodge car that was about twenty-five years old. The "senior" pastor paid himself very well and the associate pastor was living in poverty. This is another case where the pastor looks after himself first and not the people. Again, the hireling is not a shepherd of God, but is a thief and a robber.

Notice what the prophet Ezekiel foresaw long ago;

> *Then the word of the LORD came to me saying, "Son of man, prophesy against the shepherds of Israel. Prophesy and say to those shepherds, 'Thus says the Lord GOD, "Woe, shepherds of Israel who have been feeding themselves! Should not the shepherds feed the flock? "You eat the fat and clothe yourselves with the wool, you slaughter the fat sheep without feeding the flock. "Those who are sickly you have not strengthened, the diseased you have not healed, the broken you have not bound up, the scattered you have not brought back, nor have you sought for the lost; but with force and with severity you have dominated them. "**They were scattered for lack of a shepherd**, and they became food for every beast of the field and were scattered. "My flock wandered through all the mountains and on every high hill; My flock was scattered over all the surface of the earth, and there was no one to search or seek for them."""Therefore, you shepherds, hear the word of the LORD: "As I live," declares the Lord GOD, "surely because My flock has become a prey, My flock has even become food for all the beasts of the field for lack of a shepherd, and My shepherds did not search for My flock, but rather the shepherds fed themselves and did not feed My flock; therefore, you shepherds, hear the word of the LORD: '**Thus***

says the Lord GOD, "Behold, I am against the shepherds, and I will demand My sheep from them and make them cease from feeding sheep. *So the shepherds will not feed themselves anymore, but I will deliver My flock from their mouth, so that they will not be food for them.""* (Ezek. 34:1–10)

These shepherds were feeding themselves, not the sheep. They clothed themselves with wool that is fleeced from the sheep (their resources). They slaughter the fat sheep (big tithers), the ones who can support them. They slaughter them by telling them that they are going to heaven, even though they live in sin. They teach a false grace that gives a false sense of security. They preach the dead to heaven every time. The rest of the sheep that are sick with spiritual problems and they don't really heal or help them. When the lost leave the church, they don't go and bring them back and try to save them.

The broken are no better off with the divorce rate at 50 percent to 60 percent in the American church. They rule with force and severity—"if you don't like it you can leave, I am the pastor here" or "don't touch God's anointed." Because of these shepherds who took from the sheep and did nothing to heal or help them, the sheep were scattered and became food for the beast of the field (Satan and his demons). This is the condition of the church today—an institution being devoured by demons because of the hireling shepherds who preach for pay and tickle the ears of the people! So she (the "bride") has become Babylon the great harlot, a dwelling place of demons.

*And he cried out with a mighty voice, saying, "Fallen, fallen is Babylon the great! She has become a dwelling place of demons and a prison of every unclean spirit, and a prison of every unclean and hateful bird. "For all the nations have drunk of the wine of the passion of her immorality, and the kings of the earth have committed acts of immorality with her, and the **merchants of the earth have become**

> *rich by the wealth of her sensuality." I heard*
> *another voice from heaven, saying, "Come out of*
> *her, my people, so that you will not participate in*
> *her sins and receive of her plagues; for her sins have*
> *piled up as high as heaven, and God has remem-*
> *bered her iniquities. "Pay her back even as she has*
> *paid, and give back to her double according to her*
> *deeds; in the cup which she has mixed, mix twice as*
> *much for her. "To the degree that she glorified herself*
> *and lived sensuously, to the same degree give her tor-*
> *ment and mourning; for she says in her heart, 'I SIT*
> *as A QUEEN AND I AM NOT A WIDOW, and*
> *will never see mourning.' "For this reason in one*
> *day her plagues will come, pestilence and mourn-*
> *ing and famine, and she will be burned up with*
> *fire; for the Lord God who judges her is strong.*
> (Rev. 18:2–8)

She, the false bride of Christ, thinks that she will not suffer, because she thinks Jesus is her husband and will save her, but in reality, she is a harlot under judgment because she is has been going to bed with the world!

The vast majority of today's pastors are hirelings. As a result, the hirelings are elevating themselves above the rest of the members. They not only expect to be paid well, but also to be honored and treated special with titles used with or substituted for their names.

Jesus made it clear to not treat anyone special:

> *"But they do all their deeds to be noticed by men,*
> *"They love the place of honor at banquets and the*
> *chief seats in the synagogues, and respectful greetings*
> *in the market places, and being called Rabbi* (or
> Reverend) *by men. "But do not be called Rabbi* (or
> pastor)*; for One is your Teacher, and you are all*
> *brothers. "Do not call anyone on earth your father*

(as Catholic's do); for One is your Father, He who is in heaven. "Do not be called leaders (clergy)*; for One is your Leader, that is, Christ. "But the greatest among you shall be your servant. "Whoever exalts himself shall be humbled; and whoever humbles himself shall be exalted.* (Matt. 23:5–12)

These hirelings love being called "Pastor" or "Doctor" or "Reverend" just like the Pharisees loved to be called "rabbi." They love the respectful greetings wherever they go. If these men didn't want to be honored this way, they would not let people use special titles in place of their name or give them special honor. Paul was an apostle, but his name was Paul. A man can be a leader, but his name is not leader. A man could be a pastor, but his name is not pastor nor is his name preceded by "pastor" when someone speaks of him or to him. God hates these labels that separate and elevate some men above others.

And it approaches blasphemy for anyone to call a man "Father" or "Reverend" since only God is our spiritual Father and only God is to be Revered. For your information, the word reverend comes from the word revere, which means to be worshiped, revered and feared. It also indicates that one is to be honored and adored and highly respected as being most holy. This is the place only for God and not for any man. And we should only fear God and not any man. How dare any servant of God to allow anyone to address him as reverend. This very titling and honoring thing tells us that they are not really of God when they allow this to be done. According to Jesus we are all brothers. There are no men to be specially honored. *Only Jesus* is special and worthy of this kind of honor. The greatest man you will ever find is the humble man who is a servant. We are all called to be servants.

There is no such thing as the clergy. This is another title of elevation developed by men to Lord it over the rest of the flock that they have called the laity. *Neither the word clergy nor laity* are found in the Bible, nor is the application of their meanings. The "clergy" get to park in special places at the building and the sign is placed there for them. They love the best seats in the meetings and the respectful greetings wherever they go. They love the honor of men and the unjust gain they receive from the members who work for a living. They are acting more like kings and princes than like humble servants of the people. Here is the king principle—

> *He said, "This will be the procedure of the king who will reign over you: __he will take your sons and place them for himself__ in his chariots and among his horsemen and they will run before his chariots. "He will appoint for himself commanders of thousands and of fifties, and some to do his plowing and to reap his harvest and to make his weapons of war and equipment for his chariots. "He will also take your daughters for perfumers and cooks and bakers. "He will take the best of your fields and your vineyards and your olive groves and give them to his servants. "__He will take a tenth__* (tithe) *of your seed and of your vineyards and give to his officers* (staff) *and to his servants. "He will also take your male servants and your female servants and your best young men and your donkeys and use them for his work* (programs). *"He will take a tenth of your flocks, and __you yourselves will become his servants__* (doing volunteer work). (1 Sam. 8:11–17)

So the pastor/king of today will reign over you as the special leader called the "clergy" or "reverend" or "doctor" or "pastor" or "father" or "priest." He will take your sons and daughters and wives and run them in his programs (without pay). He will appoint his own elders and deacons over the members to do his will. He will use your sons and daughters for his own personal benefit. He will take the best of your time and energy for the "church" programs and different ministries. He will take a tenth of your income and call it the tithe and pay himself and pay his staff with it. And you will end up being his servant, giving your time, energy and money to him, rather than him being your servant bringing the Word of God at no cost to you and turning you from your sins to save your soul. And he will keep you too busy doing things for the church to focus on your own family or your relationship with the Lord. He will praise you and call you a "faithful" Christian because you serve him so well.

And this pastor/king will focus on numbers, dollars and programs. For example, he will expect the youth ministers to meet a quota of certain numbers or he may fire him and hire someone else to get the numbers he expects. In order for the youth minister to meet the quota, he has to water down the Word of God and entertain the young people with games and food, rather than teach them truth and the principles that would save their souls. So today's youth meetings are more about pizza, entertainment, fun, and games that provide pleasure for the kids, rather than life giving principles. The truth is that if the youth minister narrowed down the number of kids that he could really work within the things that matter, he would only have a few. This would result in him losing his job, so he won't do that. In the end the numbers matter more than souls, so the end result is that it is just business as usual.

The pastor does the same thing. He has to market to his customers. He has to keep up the numbers and of course the offerings as well. This is his measure of success, numbers and money. So he gives them what they want, not too much of that boring preaching stuff, nothing that would make them feel guilty of sin and nothing that would make them uncomfortable. His goal is to keep his customers happy and coming back for more.

If fact, he must excel in making people feel good about themselves in order to keep them coming back, even though most of them are deeply connected to the world. And of course, he must provide great entertainment for his customers, excellent music, different singers, special plays, choir songs, a few jokes, a reasonable amount of tickling of the ears and he better keep it all short, so everyone can get to lunch on time. So if the pastor makes the customers happy they will be glad to pay him and brag on him and keep coming back for more.

Notice this scripture from Paul the apostle—

> Or do you not know that **the unrighteous will not inherit the kingdom of God? Do not be deceived**; neither fornicators, nor idolaters, nor adulterers, nor **effeminate**, nor homosexuals, nor thieves, nor the covetous, nor drunkards, nor revilers, nor swindlers, will inherit the kingdom of God. (1 Col. 6:9–10)

Effeminate: The Greek word "malakos," a soft man, a man with soft hands, a man with feminine characteristics, a man unacquainted with manly work. The effeminate is NOT the same word for homosexual here, even though some homosexuals are effeminate. This Greek word *malakos* only appears four times in the Bible and is translated one time as effeminate and three times as soft in the New American Standard Bible. Let us look at the other three times from the mouth of Jesus:

> As these men were going away, Jesus began to speak to the crowds about John, "What did you go out into the wilderness to see? A reed shaken by the wind? "But what did you go out to see? **A man dressed in soft clothing**? **Those who wear soft clothing are in kings' palaces**! "But what did you go out to see? A prophet? Yes, I tell you, and one who is more than a prophet. "This is the one about whom it is written, 'BEHOLD, I SEND MY MESSENGER AHEAD OF YOU, WHO WILL PREPARE YOUR WAY BEFORE YOU.' (Matt. 11:7–10)

> When the messengers of John had left, He began to speak to the crowds about John, "What did you

*go out into the wilderness to see? A reed shaken by the wind? "But what did you go out to see? **A man dressed in soft clothing**? Those who are splendidly clothed and live in luxury are found in royal palaces! "But what did you go out to see? A prophet? Yes, I say to you, and one who is more than a prophet. "This is the one about whom it is written, 'BEHOLD, I SEND MY MESSENGER AHEAD OF YOU, WHO WILL PREPARE YOUR WAY BEFORE YOU.'* (Luke 7:24–27)

You see here that Jesus is talking about the difference between a true messenger of God like John the Baptist vs. a soft man who lives in a "king's palace," the effeminate. The king (the clergy) of our time lives in the biggest office at the church building doing no manly work to earn a living. He is typically a soft man since He doesn't do anything physical. He is following the procedure of the king that the prophet Samuel explained in first Samuel chapter 8. The effeminate preaches and collects the tithe, so he can live a soft and easy lifestyle. He also uses the members to run his programs for the church which makes him look good. He loves sordid gain—that is, the money others have worked for. This is the hireling Jesus talked about in John chapter 10, who is not the shepherd of God. He is the one who came to steal, kill and destroy. Yet he is very popular with the people.

I want to be fair, so I must include this with my remarks about the paid preacher. I have no doubt that there are a few good, decent, and godly men serving as a pastor in a few places and are presently being paid for that service. These pastors are few and far between. I am sure these men have the best interest of the people at heart and want to please God, but struggle with being totally straightforward with the people while they are supported by the same people. Since they are not greedy men, they often receive much less than they would in a secular job and therefore they are making personal sacrifice for the sake of souls. But they did not learn this practice from the Bible, but from a broken church system that has handed down traditions from men, not from God to them. If they went to Bible school or seminary, they were programed to become a paid pastor, expecting to be taken care of by the people and to be above the people as "clergy."

These good men just didn't know any better than to do as they were taught. Any paid pastor who has the right heart will read this book and reevaluate his life and method of being paid for preaching. He will look for other men in his own church who are qualified elders and teachers and share this responsibility of discipling members with them. He will get a job and move away from expensive buildings and budgets and simplify the work of the church to discipling people and saving souls, rather than building buildings and programs to keep people happy. In fact, he will move much more toward telling church members that they have no hope unless they repent of sin and become overcomers, bearing fruit and enduring to the end. He will not worry about being popular and will recognize that being paid only makes it much harder to tell the people what they really need to hear. This good pastor will hear the voice of Jesus and follow after Him and run to the truth when he hears it.

> *"No servant can serve two masters; for either he will hate the one and love the other, or else he will be devoted to one and despise the other. You cannot serve God and wealth." Now the Pharisees, who* **were lovers of money**, *were listening to all these things and were scoffing at Him. And He said to them, "You are those who justify yourselves in the sight of men, but God knows your hearts;* **for that which is highly esteemed among men is detestable in the sight of God**. (Luke 16:13–15)

If any pastor scoffs at this book, he is like the Pharisees, who were lovers of money and being honored by men. He cannot serve God and money. If the money and his position matter so much he is not fit for service in God's Kingdom. The concept of paying a preacher is highly esteemed among men but is detestable in the sight of God.

> *"Those who hate the LORD would pretend obedience to Him, And their time of punishment would be forever."* (Ps. 81:15)

Many, many, many so-called pastors, evangelist, prophets, apostles, and teachers pretend to love the Lord and pretend to obey the Lord, but if you take the money away, will they still serve the Lord? Will they still serve to disciple people and teach the Word of God for free?

> *Thus says the LORD concerning the prophets who lead my people astray; When they have something to bite with their teeth, They cry,* **"Peace,"** *But against him who puts nothing in their mouths* **They declare holy war**. (Mic. 3:5)

(It was a common practice to bite gold to make sure it was genuine.)

So here is a common scenario today—a young man feels called to preach. He really wants to help people and serve God. He is told he has to go to Bible school or seminary. So he does. There he is programmed with the "clergy" mindset and taught how he is to be above the people and how he should be taken care of by the people. He is also taught various traditions of men and numerous false doctrines. When he graduates, he is hired by a small church and begins his sincere career as a paid pastor. At first, he is all wholehearted to help everyone find God and to build up the numbers. He has to do most everything himself, preach, teach classes, oversee the Sunday school, devise programs, and take care of the budget. As the church grows, he takes in more and more money, so then there is a building program and added staff members.

The more numbers he gains the more money comes in, the easier it gets for him. Now he can delegate more of the work to other staff members and volunteers. He can take a bigger and bigger salary as the church grows and soon he is tempted more and more to compromise with members in sin and to make the messages more and more appealing to the members. Therefore, he now preaches a more ear tickling message than he did in the beginning and now doesn't want to offend anyone. As time goes on the desire for more numbers and the love of the money corrupt the pastor and he then becomes an effeminate (soft) and a hireling at heart. The larger numbers and taking in more money is how he measures his success. By this point in time there is not any church discipline to speak of and he has become a man pleaser rather than a God pleaser. Even though he was not this way in the beginning, he was set up by Satan to fall into this trap and he will end up in hell with almost all his members. You see, he was corrupted by the love of the numbers and the love of the money. These loves replaced his original love for God and the people, and he fell into the trap of the harlot church system that has devoured countless ministers and members over the centuries. And it is worse today than ever before. This is very sad and very serious.

So is the paid preacher/pastor idea as is mostly practiced today, a biblical *truth* or a *myth*?

Chapter 4

The Myth of the Worship Service

The sign in front of the "church" building reads something like this: "Worship Service" 10:00 a.m. on Sunday morning, 6:00 p.m. on Sunday evening, and 7:30 on Wednesday evening. Of course, some meet on Saturday or possibly other days of the week, but the message is still about the same.

The suggestion is that worship is something that is done in a building at some address and at some set point in time. But is this what the Bible teaches about worship for the church?

Notice what Jesus told the woman at the well:

> *The woman *said to Him, "Sir, I perceive that You are a prophet. "Our fathers worshiped in this mountain, and you people say that in Jerusalem is the place where men ought to worship." Jesus *said to her, "Woman, believe Me, __an hour is coming when neither in this mountain nor in Jerusalem will you worship the Father__. "You worship what you do not know; we worship what we know, for salvation is from the Jews. "__But an hour is coming, and now is__, when the __true worshipers will worship the Father in spirit and truth; for such people the Father seeks to be His worshipers. "God is spirit, and those who wor-__*

ship Him must worship in spirit and truth."
(John 4:19–24)

So obviously Jesus was speaking of a time when the old outward form of worship would end. Of course, the time He was referring to, was the time of His death on the cross when the ordinances of the law would be nailed to the cross and the new church age would begin. The old form of outward worship included having to go to a temple or building or some other "sacred" place in order to worship. There, at that location, certain outward things would be done, like physical sacrifices would be made as well as certain rituals performed. There also could be singing as well as bowing or the lifting of hands. Whatever was done was a physical act done in a physical location and at a certain time appointed for the service, but the problem now is that men have brought the old form of worship back and have, again, let the traditions of men invalidate and make to no effect the Word of God.

So what is it to worship in spirit and truth and where and when should that take place?

> *Therefore I urge you, brethren, by the mercies of God,* *to present your bodies a living and holy sacrifice, acceptable to God, which is your spiritual service of worship. And do not be conformed to this world, but be transformed by the renewing of your mind, so that you may prove what the will of God is, that which is good and acceptable and perfect.* (Rom. 12:1–2)

So nothing you can do at "church" on Sunday can substitute for presenting your body as a living and holy sacrifice to be acceptable to God as your spiritual service of worship on a daily basis. This is to be done in and from the heart at all times, seven days a week. You can't go to some building on certain occasions in order to do this. It is a heart thing, a matter of the heart, not some outward religious ceremony or physical act that God wants.

So where is the house of God and where is the temple located now?

> *Or what agreement has the temple of God with idols?* ***For we are the temple of the living God;*** *just as God said, "I WILL DWELL IN THEM AND WALK AMONG THEM; AND I WILL BE THEIR GOD, AND THEY SHALL BE MY PEOPLE.* (2 Col. 6:16)

So we are the temple of God and therefore worship must take place inside us, in our hearts, not in a building or some other place where we have to go and do something outward.

> *Or do you not know that* ***your body is a temple*** *of the Holy Spirit who is in you, whom you have from God, and that you are not your own? For you have been bought with a price:* ***therefore, glorify God in your body***. (1 Co. 6:19–20)

Again, our bodies are the temple and the only place of worship to God. And we are to offer up our bodies in holy living, at all times. This is the service of worship that God wants, to offer up ourselves to Him daily rather than give him some traditions on Sunday, done over and over again by rote/repetition week after week. The Lord is sick of all that. He wants a heart that is totally His, not the same old religious outward "worship" offered up to him week after week the same way over and over again. This is just meaningless repetition and is not of the Spirit and truth.

> *And a lawyer stood up and put Him to the test, saying, "Teacher, what shall I do to inherit eternal life?" And He said to him, "What is written in the Law? How does it read to you?" And he*

> *answered,* "**YOU SHALL LOVE THE LORD YOUR GOD WITH ALL YOUR HEART, AND WITH ALL YOUR SOUL, AND WITH ALL YOUR STRENGTH, AND WITH ALL YOUR MIND; AND YOUR NEIGHBOR AS YOURSELF**." *And He said to him, "You have answered correctly; DO THIS AND YOU WILL LIVE."* (Luke 10:25–28)

Here, He is referring to what it takes to have eternal life!

You worship God when you love Him with all your heart. This is done by the Spirit and not by an outward singing of a song on Sunday or any other outward act. What is done by the Spirit is that which is from the heart, inside the heart and carried out in the body daily.

> *"Do not think that I came to bring peace on the earth;* **I did not come to bring peace, but a sword**. *"For I came to SET A MAN AGAINST HIS FATHER, AND A DAUGHTER AGAINST HER MOTHER, AND A DAUGHTER-IN-LAW AGAINST HER MOTHER-IN-LAW; and A MAN'S ENEMIES WILL BE THE MEMBERS OF HIS HOUSEHOLD. "*He who loves father or mother more than Me is not worthy of Me; and he who loves son or daughter more than Me is not worthy of Me*. (Matt. 10:34–37)

You worship Him when you love Him more than your family!

You worship the Lord in Spirit and truth when you refuse to love any family member more than the Lord. When anyone really turns to the Lord with all his heart and he begins to practice righteous living, then some of his ungodly family members will turn against him for his stand for what is right. This is why Jesus said He did not come to bring peace. There will be trouble in the family when anyone gives God his whole heart. If you compromise for the sake of peace or because you love father or mother or son or daughter more, you are not worthy of Him. Most so-called "Christians" today never worship the Lord by loving Him more than family.

It is much easier to go to church at "worship" time and sing a few songs, than to take a righteous stand with family members who are close to you. Jesus promised you division in your family if you gave your whole heart to Him. He knew it would require sacrifice on your part, but few are really willing to be rejected by family because of the Lord and His standards of living. Therefore, their worship consists of tradition learned by rote and their heart is far from pleasing the Lord in this matter.

> *"And **he who does not take his cross and follow after Me is not worthy of Me**. "He who has found his life will lose it, and he who has lost his life for My sake will find it.* (Matt. 10:38–39)

You worship the Lord when you take up your cross and follow after Jesus. Your cross is your cross, not the cross of Jesus. It seems that every denomination mostly talks about the cross of Jesus, but rarely, if almost never, does any pastor teach about your cross. Your cross is the place of your suffering, the place of your death to self and to sin. Your cross is the place where you deny yourself of worldly pleasures and deeds of the flesh. Your cross is the place where you give up your old life for His sake. If you don't give up your old life now, you will not have heaven with the Lord later. To bear your own cross is another way you worship the Lord in Spirit and truth.

> *And He was saying to them all, "If anyone wishes to come after Me, he must deny himself, and **take up his cross daily** and follow Me.* (Luke 9:23)

Again, you can't even think about following Jesus unless you deny yourself and take up "your" cross daily. Jesus had His cross and you have your cross to bear. Jesus is not going in the direction of any sin or the ways of the world. He is not participating in the idolatry of the world. He is not involved in gossip, divorce, lust, deception, anger, jealously, impurity, pornography, adultery, immorality, drunkenness, or anything like these. So no one can follow Jesus without taking up his cross and denying himself of sin in all forms, since Jesus is not going in that direction. You can't live like the rest of the world and then go to church on Sunday and sing, "O, how I love Jesus" and think you have worshiped God. Unless you are taking up your own cross daily and dying daily to your selfish ways, you are not worshiping God, no matter how loud you sing at church.

> *I affirm, brethren, by the boasting in you which I have in Christ Jesus our Lord, I **die daily**.* (1 Col. 15:31)

Paul understood this very well. He died daily. This was his spiritual service of worship to the Lord God Almighty. To offer up himself to the Lord daily by denying self of sin and the world and even his own will. Paul knew he did not have to wait for some church to open and have a "worship service" in order to worship the Lord. Paul did it in Spirit and truth daily.

I once had a greedy false pastor tell me that he knew how to start a church and have many people come quickly and have great financial success with it. I asked him how he would be able to do that. He said it is the music; it is all about the music program!

He explained that having a great assembly of good musicians with a well-trained choir would be very appealing to lots of people. He also told me that the preaching should be comforting and not too long to make the people feel better about going to church.

But here is the question—what has music, choir or singing to do with worship to the Lord?

> *There is not one record in the New Testament where any of the churches had a worship service, a minister*

of music, a choir, a worship leader, a musical band, or even a song leader. It is just not there. So how is it that virtually every church today has most, if not all these things and call the music and singing worship? This did not come from the Bible, so where did it come from? The Bible has made it clear that worship is something done in and from the heart daily and not at some building somewhere at a specified time. Again, do you see how the traditions of men have taken over and how the worship of today consists of traditions learned by rote and is far from the will and heart of God?

Since worship is a heart matter, who can "lead" you in it. If it is not motivated from within your own heart to obey God, do the right thing, acknowledge God, thank God, forgive others, deny yourself of sin, take up your cross, etc. Then is it not phony, empty and meaningless? Is it not just going through the motions? Who can lead your heart, except you and your own willingness to allow the Spirit of God to do so?

So what is a worship leader? All he can do is to tell you to stand and sing the first and third verses or to sit and then stand again. Up and down doing what "Simon says." Everyone is doing the same thing at the same time the same way, like programmed robots. Do you really think this is what God wants? Do you really think this is worship in Spirit and truth? Do you really think that a human can lead you to worship from the heart? This is why no worship leaders existed in the New Testament church. Worship must be done in Spirit and truth in the heart which is the true temple, rather than in a building. It is total nonsense to think that you could be led into true worship by another person since it is an individual heart thing done by the will of that person and led by the Holy Spirit from inside that person. True worship is not some outward thing that can be controlled by another human being telling you to sing or clap or sit or stand.

So what about singing? There is nothing wrong with singing as long as we don't make someone think it is worship to God. But singing is just singing. It can be edifying and that is a good thing, but the Bible does not define true worship as singing. There certainly is no law against singing. Someone could even be worshiping the Lord from the heart while they were singing, but the singing itself is not defined as worship. But what has happened now is that singing has been made into a substitution for true worship causing people to believe that when they sing, they have worshiped God, which is totally false. But there is some instruction about speaking psalms and hymns to each other:

> *And do not get drunk with wine, for that is dissipation, but be filled with the Spirit, __speaking__ to one another in psalms and hymns and spiritual songs, singing and making melody __with your heart__ to the Lord; always giving thanks for all things in the name of our Lord Jesus Christ to God, even the Father; and be subject to one another in the fear of Christ.* (Eph. 5:18–21)

Here the spiritual songs were to be making melody with our hearts to the Lord. And that we should be *SPEAKING* to one another the psalms, hymns, and spiritual songs we have (which are in our heart), while always giving thanks and being subject to one another in the fear of the Lord. This song is not found in a hymn book or on an overhead projector. This song is only found in the heart of a true worshiper. This is not the type of songs found in most every church week after week around the world.

> *What is the outcome then, brethren? When you assemble, __each one__ has a psalm, has a teaching, has a revelation, has a tongue, has an interpretation. Let all things be done for edification.* (1 Col. 14:26)

Again, there is no corporate worship service here with a song leader. Each person, each individual comes with something to give. *One* has a psalm to give for edification. Someone else has a revelation. Someone else has a teaching, etc. Not everyone is doing the same thing at the same time. If someone has a song to sing for edification, then let that person speak it or sing it. If another has a teaching for edification, then let him teach. These gifts and services offered are done on an individual basis for the common good, one gift at a time, not the way we see the "worship services" done today. Again, tradition rules rather than the Word of God.

> *Let the word of Christ richly dwell within you, with all wisdom teaching and admonishing* (giving warning) *one another with psalms and hymns and spiritual songs, singing with thankfulness* **in your hearts to God**. (Col. 3:16)

Here the instruction that precedes your spiritual hymn or song, is to first let the Word of Christ richly dwell within you. Once the Word richly dwells within you, then you are to teach and admonish one another with psalms and hymns and spiritual songs while singing with thankfulness in your heart. The singing is done in your heart while you are teaching and admonishing one another with your psalms and hymns and spiritual songs. Teaching the Word of God is to give instruction and admonishing is to give warnings to God's people. Be honest here, where does this happen today? What denomination practices this—to speak psalms, hymns, and spiritual songs as a way of teaching and warning to God's people? Did you ever read the song God gave to Moses to write and speak to the children of Israel in Deuteronomy chapter 31? It was filled with warnings and teachings for the people of God. Why do we not have this today? Does your worship service of singing songs picked out by a song leader and being told what to sing and when to sing look anything like what the Word of God says a song should be from the heart?

*Now may the God who gives perseverance and encouragement grant you to be of the **same mind** with one another according to Christ Jesus, so that with **one accord** you may with **one voice** glorify the God and Father of our Lord Jesus Christ.*
(Rom. 15:5–6)

Here is how the church can produce the beautiful sound the Lord really wants, to be of the same mind, to be in one accord and have one voice and to be in agreement with each other. That means no divisions (not thousands of denominations). Also, on a local church basis, it means no quarrels, strife, jealously or unforgiveness among you. Can you imagine how much of an abomination it is to the Lord to have church members angry, bitter, jealous, or hating one another while all standing together and singing "O, how I love Jesus" during "worship" at church? Or having members in willful sin singing praises to the Lord as the minister of music directs them. This is the condition of almost all of the so-called worship services that go on week after week and virtually no one even questions it. The Lord must be thoroughly disgusted with it all. Again, tradition rules rather than the will of God.

*To sum up, all of you be **harmonious**, sympathetic, brotherly, kindhearted, and humble in spirit; not returning evil for evil or insult for insult, but giving a blessing instead; for you were called for the very purpose that you might inherit a blessing.*
(1 Pet. 3:8–9)

Again, the Lord desires a church that is in harmony together. We are the instruments that make a joyful sound to the Lord, not pianos or guitars. It should come from our hearts, not a building. God is a Spirit, not flesh and blood. He listens with spiritual ears to the sounds that come from within our hearts, not just by sound waves that strike the ear drum as a physical man has. God hears if we are grumbling, angry, jealous, lusting, sinning, bitter, or if we are anything but harmonious with each other or with Him from within our hearts. There is no way you can go to church and sing a few songs and say you have worshiped God if you have anything wrong in your heart with your spouse, your brother, your neighbor or with God. If you are right with God and you have truly worshiped him in Spirit and truth all week, then you have no need to sing a few songs at church on Sunday or Saturday, for you have given the Lord what he really wants—your adoration from the heart and obedience to His Word. This is your spiritual service of worship, to offer up your body as a living sacrifice daily! Singing at church can never substitute for that.

> *Now I exhort you, brethren, by the name of our Lord Jesus Christ, that **you all agree** and that there be **no divisions** among you, but that you be made complete in the **same mind and in the same judgment**.* (1 Col. 1:10)

It should be clear by now what the Lord really wants. The song He wants is for the church (his people) to be in harmony, one voice, one faith, one gospel, one church, in agreement, one mind, one body, common doctrines, bearing fruit, living righteous by being obedient while taking up their cross daily and denying self of worldly desires. If this song is sung and this worship takes place, you will have no need to go to a certain building somewhere at a certain time to "worship," because you will be worshiping in Spirit and truth already.

Remember that the modern American Christian church is full of sin and worldliness. Today's church uses grace as a license for sin and teaches the easy escape doctrine of the rapture. It also teaches unconditional eternal security and the false doctrine of salvation by "sinner's prayer" rather than repentance for forgiveness of sin. It's no wonder the church is full of sin. The narrow way has been eliminated by modern paid pastors, and now this modern church that is so full of sin teaches its members that they can appease their conscience and please God by singing a few songs on Sunday and it is called a "worship service."

This is such an insult to the Almighty Creator who is far more intelligent than every human on earth put together. To suggest that He just wants us to gather and sing a few songs for him on Sunday as if we were robots being led by a "worship leader" is mindless. It's such a lie, such a falsehood to teach people that this super intelligent God wants something so superficial and meaningless as man-made worship, rather than having our hearts and obedience and love for Him. So here is how the Lord feels about man-made worship that substitutes for what He really wants from His people.

> *"**I hate, I reject** your festivals, **Nor, do I delight in your solemn assemblies**. "Even though you offer up to Me burnt offerings and your grain offerings, **I will not accept** them; And I will not even look at the peace offerings of your fatlings. "**Take away from Me the noise of your songs; I will not even listen to the sound of your harps**. "But let **justice** roll down like waters And **righteousness** like an ever-flowing stream.* (Amos 5:21–24)

The Lord absolutely hates church meetings with the rituals and ceremonies men offer to him while justice and righteousness are missing. He said take away from Him the NOISE of your songs and He said He would not listen to your musical instruments. He HATES this: to come together to sing and make music when sin and worldliness is not addressed, and to call the superficial singing and playing of instruments a "worship service" when God never instructed the church to worship in this way. The Lord wants all of our hearts and for us to love Him and to obey Him completely. If we do that it is enough, IT IS ENOUGH! He will be well pleased! So please don't insult Him with a superficial man-made worship service used to substitute for wholehearted love and obedience to Him. No one can lead you to worship In Spirit and truth except the Holy Spirit. There is no physical location to go for worship and it is not something to be done at a set time. It is the total surrender of your life to Jesus and your full repentance from sin and complete obedience to His Word done every day at all times and in every place you go. When you take up your cross and deny yourself of worldly desires and follow Him with all your heart, you are offering up your body as a living sacrifice and dying daily to self, which is your reasonable service of worship. This is worshiping in Spirit and truth and nothing you can do at a church meeting can substitute for this true worship!

Most people who attend church have a love affair with the "worship service" rather than with the Lord. They love the music, the choir, the band, the orchestra, the traditional hymns, or the contemporary modern songs along with the rituals and ceremonies. There are now "Christian" radio stations devoted to mainly playing "Christian" music with virtually no teaching of the word of God, just music, music, and more music. A lot of the music is patterned after the world's rock and roll. They try to sanitize it by calling it "Christian rock."

These "Christian" rockers offer concerts where "Christian" music artists come to play and sing for the people's pleasure. This is very popular and is highly esteemed among the people, but it is mostly without any serious call to repentance and without addressing the sins of the church members who come to hear their music. If there was any kind of preaching done there like the way Jesus, Paul, or John the Baptist did, most of the people would be highly offended and greatly disappointed and want their money back because they came to worship the music, not God, nor did they come to hear and obey His word. Not only do the people come to bow down and to worship the music, but also the musicians and singers. These so-called "Christian" artists often arrive in a limousine much like the rock stars of the world do, with the "Christian" fans screaming and applauding them like they were some kind of gods. And these "celebrities" allow the people to treat them in such a way as is only deserved by the Lord Jesus Christ. It is obvious where the object of worship is, the music and the musician, not the Lord God Almighty! He said, "You shall have no other gods before me," and He meant it.

Notice this. The so-called "Christian artists" are making a very good living from the concerts and the sales of their music CDs. Many have become very rich. Again, didn't we hear somewhere that whatever we have received, we received it freely and shouldn't we freely give it. Have we forgotten what Jesus did in the temple, turning over the money changers tables and whipping them out of the temple, because they were selling the so-called objects of worship? He called them a den of robbers. Why should we think it is any different today, selling our "spiritual" gifts for money? This is just another way of "selling" what is called the gospel/gospel music.

Most of the so-called worship is nothing more than entertainment for the flesh. Something that keeps people coming back week after week because they enjoy it. The Charismatics and Pentecostals often sing for very long periods of time and it seems to put the people into a hypnotic, emotional trance. They call it high praise. The Catholics swing incense pots and the Lutherans sing in a very stiff and formal manner. The Church of Christ sings only acapella and the nondenominational churches have bands with drums and many other instruments.

The Presbyterians and Episcopalians read their prayers from a book of common prayer and the Baptist promote the choir music more than most others. All these different forms of "worship" are man-made and none of them are found in the instructions of the New Testament for the church. As a result, we have countless so-called Christians who have been deceived into believing that they are worshiping God when they participate in these various forms of so-called worship. They think that they have to go to the "church building" and be led by some man and either sing or listen to the choir in order to worship God. They have been deceived into believing that worship takes place somewhere and at a certain time and led by someone. Shouldn't we check with the Lord and see how He feels about all this so-called worship? Well, the Lord has spoken through his prophets, Jesus and Paul. And he hates it, especially when justice and righteousness are not practiced by His people. The songs of this church today are nothing more than just a noisy gong or a clanging cymbal to the Lord and He hates it because His people no longer fear Him and no longer offer up their lives in true worship to Him. America and its churches have been taken over by Satan.

Second Peter 2 says that the false prophets lead the people by their fleshly desires and by sensuality. Contemporary Christian music does just that. The worship service is now worshiped, rather than the Lord. The music is desired more than righteousness. If you remove the music program from virtually any church today, it would dry up quickly. The music is used to manipulate the members into certain moods to accomplish the purposes of the church leaders. Some of the main moods are the giving mood or the alter call mood or the pull to support a special program or "good work" mood. Music is powerful and used by church leaders for mood control. This has gone on for centuries.

> *"**It shall come about if you ever forget the LORD your God and go after other gods and serve them and worship them, I testify against you today that you will surely perish**. "Like the nations that the LORD makes to perish before you, so you shall perish; because you would not listen to the voice of the LORD your God.* (Deut. 8:19–20)

So just to be clear again, worship is not singing or making music. Singing is singing, and music is music. Worship is what your heart goes after and the god you serve from within. If your god is money, you don't gather people around you and get a band of musical instruments to make music and sing songs about money in order to worship the god of money, do you?

Of course not, you just practice greed from your heart. Neither do you worship the one and only true and living God in that way, using music. The way you worship other gods is to give them your heart, your affection, your love, your devotion and you do everything in your everyday life you can to satisfy your desire for that god. It doesn't matter if that god is pride, sex, lust, greed, selfishness, anger, jealously, sports, money, or any one of many of other gods offered by this world every day. If you worship and serve the god of sexual lust, you do so from within your heart every time you entertain lustful thoughts or commit immoral acts or view sexual content or participate in dirty jokes.

You don't have to sing songs about lust in order to worship the god of sexual lust, just serve it from within your heart. So it is the same with the Lord God, you worship Him when you choose to please Him in your day to day life in all the ways you do business, treat others, work, think, and conduct yourself as you obey Him. There is no temple or church building you can go to for this kind of true worship service. You are the temple of God and true worship takes place in your heart at all times and at every location as you walk with God and serve Him with your life and from your heart. No church service can substitute for true worship and no building can substitute for your heart (the true temple of God) and no outward act can substitute for love and obedience toward God from the heart.

> *Or what agreement has the temple of God with idols?* *For we are the temple of the living God; just as God said, "I WILL DWELL IN THEM AND WALK AMONG THEM; AND I WILL BE THEIR GOD, AND THEY SHALL BE MY PEOPLE. "Therefore, COME OUT FROM THEIR MIDST AND BE SEPARATE," says the Lord. "AND DO NOT TOUCH WHAT IS UNCLEAN; And I will welcome you. "And I will be a father to you, And you shall be sons and daughters to Me," Says the Lord Almighty.*
> (2 Col. 6:16–18)

I have noticed that many so-called "Christians" have idols. Idols are things that you love more than God. Things your heart takes more interest in and care for, more than God.

I have been to men's Bible studies where the main topic being discussed was about sports before and after the meeting. This shows that, in their hearts, they are more interested in sports than in talking about the Lord or His Word. It is amazing to me that so many men who claim to know God, know far less about the Bible than they do about sports celebrities who are paid millions of dollars per year to entertain them. These sports lovers can quote the history of the players and games and give amazing statistics on how many hits, kicks, yards gained, games won, games lost, players scores, and even give predictions of who will win the major playoffs, etc. Yet rarely do I find even one "Christian" man who can lead someone to the Lord from the Scriptures without bringing that person to his pastor or maybe Sunday school teacher for help. For someone who claims to be a Christian to know so little about God/His Word and so much about sports, shows that his god is sports and that he is worshiping and serving an idol/another god. And in the same way, another god is so often the worship music, the worship service.

Here is some more about true worship:

> *For You do not delight in sacrifice, otherwise I would give it; You are not pleased with burnt offering.* ***The sacrifices of God are a broken spirit; A broken and a contrite heart, O God, You will not despise****.* (Ps. 51:16)

What if we as a nation stopped offering these superficial sacrifices of "worship" to God each week and began to repent of our sins as a "Christian" nation and returned to the Lord in brokenness for our sins, for serving other gods, for being lukewarm, for compromising with the world, for our lack of wholeheartedness, for our lack of serious seeking of the Lord and for our shallow superficial "Christianity"? What if we actually became the church rather than just going to church? What if we as a nation really worshiped the Lord Jesus Christ truly in Spirit and truth? What if we had real revival in all the churches? What if we laid down the traditions of men and obeyed the Word of God and truly worshiped God in Spirit and truth?

A few final thoughts:

> Jesus said, *"**If you love Me, you will keep My commandments**. "He who has My commandments and keeps them is the one who loves Me; and he who loves Me will be loved by My Father, and I will love him and will disclose Myself to him." Jesus answered and said to him, "**If anyone loves Me, he will keep My word; and My Father will love him**, and We will come to him and **make Our abode with him**. "He who does not love Me does not keep My words; and the word which you hear is not Mine, but the Father's who sent Me.* (John 14:15, 21, 23, 24)

Worship in Spirit and truth is very simple. You must love God, love His Word, and obey Him from the heart. If you love Him, you will do what He says. If you don't do what He says, you don't love Him. If you don't love Him and don't obey Him, no doctrine or church service can keep you out of hell. If you don't do what He says, you are not worshiping Him. If you are obeying Him, you are already worshiping Him.

To love Him, to appreciate Him, to be thankful for what He has done for you, to adore Him, to fear Him, to believe Him, to seek Him, to study His word, to cry out to Him in prayer, to see Him in the creation, to speak well of Him to others, to bring others to Him, to stand against sin, to separate yourself from the ways of the world, to take up your cross daily, to live for the eternal rather than the temporal, to expose false religion, to teach the truth to others, to trust in Him with all your heart, to endure to the end, etc.—this is what true worship in Spirit and truth looks like! Nothing else you can do will substitute for what He wants and requires if you are to please Him and make it to heaven.

Under the law, worship was physical and outward. Under Jesus it is now inward and of the heart. Worship was a ritual, mechanical and physical. Now it is spiritual coming from the heart. The temple was a physical building. Now we are the temple. Our heart is the house of God. The songs sung in the past were outward. The songs now are spiritual, inward of the heart. Under the law, worship was done corporately, directed by the Levitical priest. In Jesus, it is done individually from the heart, led by the Holy Spirit as we live our lives daily.

> *But realize this, that in the last days difficult times will come. For men will be lovers of self, lovers of money, boastful, arrogant, revilers, disobedient to parents, ungrateful, unholy, unloving, irreconcilable, malicious gossips, without self-control, brutal, haters of good, treacherous, reckless, conceited, lovers of pleasure rather than lovers of God, **holding to a form of godliness, although they have denied its power**; Avoid such men as these.* (2 Tim. 3:1–5)

Today, the form of godliness is church attendance and man-made worship. This appears to be good but has no power over sin or the influence of the world. You can't sing your way to heaven. You must worship Him in Spirit and truth or you will be lost forever! So who or what do you worship? The Lord will not be one of your many idols. You must love Him with all your heart or He will not accept you. It does not matter if you belong to a church, got baptized and did some good things. If He is not Lord of all your heart, He will not be your Lord at all. Check yourself. Where are your main affections? What do you cherish the most? Where is your mind most of the time? Is your delight in the Word of God and the things of God? Do you mediate upon Him and His Word day and night? Do you pray each day and often with passion and tears to the Living God? Do you fear the Lord? Do you grieve over the condition of the church and this country? Do you hunger and thirst for righteousness? Do you earnestly seek the Lord in Bible study and prayer? Do you try to save the lost? Do you open up your home to share the Word of God with others? Do you teach your family the Word of God? Do you repent quickly if you happen to sin? Do you always make any fault right with others? Do you have integrity and always speak the truth? The true worshipers do! Do you live more for the temporal or for the eternal? Everyone is worshiping something or someone, who or what do you worship?

If your answers are not too favorable to the questions just posed, you may be found to be worshiping the Lord in vain. If your heart is far from Him, you are lost and the only hope you have is to run to Jesus and repent. No religion or church membership will save you. The way really is narrow, and the gate is small that leads to life, and few are those who find it. I encourage you to give your whole heart and life to the Lord without delay and flee from the false religion and false worship that you have trusted in and do so while you still have time.

So is the modern method of Christian worship a biblical *truth* or a *myth*?

Chapter 5

The Myth of Many Being Saved

It seems that here in the "Bible belt" of the south, that most everyone claims to be a "Christian." There are approximately 43 million Baptists worldwide as well as 1.2 billion Catholics and 66 million Lutherans. And a large percentage of those numbers are here in America. That is only considering three of the major denominations. If you included all the many, many other denominations you would have to realize there are many more millions that claim to be "Christian."

Now, if all those were really true born-again Christians, wouldn't the world be a much better place than it is now? It would be if every so-called Christian really loved and obeyed God and walked in purity and righteousness before the Lord! I mean, if each one loved God with all his heart and loved his neighbor as himself, and if each "saved" person only led one other person to Jesus every ten years, just imagine how quickly the whole world would have been converted by now. The many millions of already "saved," leading another set of many millions every ten years to Jesus and then all the original and now converted many millions repeating that again every ten years over and over again. If these were real Christians and they were sowing the good seed of the Word of God as Jesus called us all to do, then the many millions would become a number in the hundreds of millions in just a few decades. But that hasn't happened. Instead, we have major denominations filled with people in sin.

Divorce is rampant in the American churches as well as immorality and pornography. Most members are so worldly, that when they are outside the church building, it is very difficult if not impossible to tell the so-called "Christian" from the average person on the street who makes no claim to God. It is obvious that the reason why the entertainment industry has gotten so vulgar and violent in recent years is because the millions and millions of so-called Christians support and enjoy the garbage they produce. And the reason they do this is because they don't belong to God or have His Spirit in them even though they usually attend church somewhere to "worship" God. The Church is supposed to be salt and light to the world. But the church today, for the most part is far from God, has no power to influence the world around it. But instead the world has had a tremendous influence on the church. Jesus said that if the salt became tasteless that it should be thrown out and trampled underfoot, and if the church has no light then it is filled with darkness. It may have nice buildings with fine furniture, stained glass windows and beautiful orchestras, but because it is devoid of the Holy Spirit and the living and abiding Word of God, it is full of darkness. Therefore, she has become a dwelling place of demons as described in Revelation chapter 18.

> *And He summoned the crowd with His disciples, and said to them, "__If anyone wishes to come after Me, he must deny himself, and take up his cross and follow Me__. "For whoever wishes to save his life will lose it, but whoever loses his life for My sake and the gospel's will save it. "For what does it profit a man to gain the whole world, and forfeit his soul? "For what will a man give in exchange for his soul?* (Mark 8:34–37)

Jesus said, if *ANYONE* wishes to come after Him, he must deny himself, take up his cross and follow Him. Anyone includes you and me and everyone else. Jesus is not going in the way of man-made religion. Jesus is not a Baptist or Catholic or Charismatic or any other of the many named groups. Jesus is the exact representation of His Father and is only going in the way of righteousness and holiness. He is not participating in any kind of sin or any kind of worldly idols, or any kind of man-made religion, or any kind of outward "worship," nor is He willing to compromise for the sake of any earthly family member. He is only going to please His heavenly father and we should only live to please Jesus and that means to worship Him in Spirit and truth by refusing to practice sin and by denying ourselves of worldly pleasures and to live righteously and godly lives here and now on the earth.

So does the Word of God support the theory of many being saved? Jesus said,

> *"Enter through the **narrow** gate; for the gate is wide and the way is broad that leads to destruction, and there are many who enter through it. "For the **gate is small** and the **way is narrow** that leads to life, and there are **few** who find it."* (Mat 7:13–14)

If you look up the meaning of the word "few" in the Greek, it means a small number, little amount or slight quantity, and the meanings for the words "narrow way" and "small gate" are difficulty, trouble, suffering, tribulation, and pain. This is referring to the suffering that all true believers experience when following Jesus with a whole heart. It is the cross that true believers must bear if they are truly His disciples. It is the rejection they will experience from family, friends, "so-called Christians" and the world in general. When anyone embarks on living a holy life, they will be persecuted especially by the religious community because the main stream church teaches a false grace with no cross of self-denial and that sinning is normal for a Christian.

> *Indeed, **all who desire to live godly in Christ Jesus will be persecuted**.* (2 Tim. 3:12)

The key here is the desire to live *GODLY*. Godly does not mean church attendance and outward "worship." Godly means being holy and separated from the world's ways and no longer participating in the same things you used to do and that your family and friends still do. When you take a stand for righteousness, your denomination, your religious family, your religious friends as well as your non-religious family and friends will turn against you. Especially when you expose the false teachings that teach salvation without repentance from sin. And when you speak about the narrow way of suffering and that you have to bear your own cross and overcome sin and temptation, you will be rejected.

Also, the Greek word here for "many" is referring to a very large number, multitudes, and multitudes of people. Kind of like the millions and millions going to church week after week without wholehearted obedience to God while they go through the outward motions of so-called worship without an inward transformation of being conformed into the image of Jesus. What they are conformed into is the denomination they belong to. If Baptist, they are conformed into a Baptist, if Catholic, they are conformed into a Catholic and if Charismatic, they are conformed into a Charismatic, etc. But none of these conformities are the image of Jesus, but all are of another spirit and another image. None of those images are like each other and certainly they are not like Jesus. If they were the image of Jesus, they would all look and sound and be alike, but since they are different, very different, they are not of God, but are of the broad way.

This scripture makes it very clear that few, very few will be willing to suffer the difficulty of their own cross that comes with truly following Jesus with a whole heart. It certainly is not millions and millions. It is just a few in number very, very few!

Jesus also said,

> *And someone said to Him, "**Lord, are there just a few who are being saved**?" And He said to them, "**Strive to enter through the narrow door**; for*

many, I tell you, will seek to enter and **will not be able**. (Luke 13:23–24)

Again, this doesn't sound like very many are going to be saved. Certainly not millions and billions. The disciples of Jesus sensed that the way to life was narrow with a small gate and with a cross to bear. They also sensed that not many were really going to be saved when they asked the question, "Lord, are there just a few who are being saved?"

Your family and friends won't mind you going to church as long as you don't really change. You won't be rejected by them as a church goer as long as you enjoy the same worldly pleasures with them as you always did before, like dirty jokes or gossip about other family members or bowing down to the god of sports or drinking or smoking that you may have once done with them. Maybe you have a hard time thinking that you could be rejected by your family by serving the Lord with a whole heart. If you really give your whole heart to the Lord and stop participating in their worldly talk and you stop laughing at their dirty jokes and you give up drinking and smoking and turn from the idols they love and you find better things to do with your time than spending countless hours watching sports with your family, you will find yourself being rejected and persecuted. Especially now that you want to talk about Jesus and His Word and what He really wants from His people.

> *"Do not think that I came to bring peace on the earth; I did not come to bring peace, but a sword. "For I came to SET A MAN AGAINST HIS FATHER, AND A DAUGHTER AGAINST HER MOTHER, AND A DAUGHTER-IN-LAW AGAINST HER MOTHER-IN-LAW; and A MAN'S ENEMIES WILL BE THE MEMBERS OF HIS HOUSEHOLD. "He who loves father or mother more than Me is not worthy of Me; and he who loves son or daughter more than Me is not worthy of Me. "And he*

who does not take his cross and follow after Me is not worthy of Me. "He who has found his life will lose it, and he who has lost his life for My sake will find it. (Matt. 10:34–39)

So here you have it. Jesus did not plan on you having peace with your family if you followed Him. In fact, if you claim to be a Christian and you don't have conflict with your worldly family, you are not really following Him. It is the *intention* of Jesus to bring a sword between you and your worldly family members. He did not intend for you to have peace with them after you came to Him. This is to test you to see if you will love Him more or love them more. He plainly said that if you love your father or mother or son or daughter more than Him you are not worthy of Him. The way you love them more than God is to compromise the ways and truth of God so as to not offend them or make them like you less. If you love them more, then you are denying the Lord by your compromises with them and disqualify yourself for eternal life.

He said that if you lose your life (the life you had with your family, friends, and the world) for His sake, you will find life. If you don't, you won't see life, even though you may go to church each week and "praise and worship" God outwardly as already described in chapter 4. You will still end up in hell forever and forever. To most people, family is an idol. This is not a small matter. We must love God with all our heart and all our soul and all our strength and with all our mind or we will not enter eternal life. The way really is very narrow and only a few really find eternal life.

> *And He was saying to them all, "If anyone wishes to come after Me,* **he must deny himself, and take up his cross daily and follow Me**. *"For who-ever wishes to save his life will lose it, but whoever loses his life for My sake, he is the one who will save it. "For what is a man profited if he gains*

the whole world, and loses or forfeits himself?
(Luke 9:23–25)

Again, consider how few are really following Jesus and how many are following man-made religion! Who is really teaching the church that if they don't take up their cross and deny themselves and give up their life for His sake that they cannot be His disciple, much less get to heaven?

> *"If anyone comes to Me and does not hate his own father and mother and wife and children and brothers and sisters, yes, and even his own life,* **_he cannot be My disciple_**. **_"Whoever does not carry his own cross and come after Me cannot be My disciple_**. *"For which one of you, when he wants to build a tower, does not first sit down and calculate the cost to see if he has enough to complete it?* (Luke 14:26–28)

Here is the cost. Give up your life as you knew it before. Be born again to a new life. Accept the division of your family and friends as you walk closer and closer to God. It is not that you should reject them, but they will reject you if you do what is right. You must carry your own cross of suffering when your family and friends reject you for His name sake. If you don't calculate the cost, you may not be able to finish the course to heaven. If you follow the modern teachings of the church today you surely will miss heaven because the cross, suffering, persecution, and repentance from sin is all left out. And if these are left out, how do you think you can make it to heaven? Do you see yet, what it is to worship in Spirit and truth and do you think you can just go to church and sing a few songs and please the Lord without giving up your life completely to Him? What does He really want from you?

As you read this are you getting any fear of God on you? Are you understanding how narrow the way to life really is? Are you coming under conviction or are you offended?

Paul the apostle warned the church with these words:

> *But immorality or any impurity or greed must not even be named among you, as is proper among saints; and there must be no filthiness and silly talk, or coarse jesting, which are not fitting, but rather giving of thanks. **For this you know with certainty**, that no immoral or impure person or covetous man, who is an idolater, has an inheritance in the kingdom of Christ and God. **Let no one deceive you with empty words**, for because of these things the wrath of God comes upon the sons of disobedience. Therefore, do not be partakers with them; for you were formerly darkness, but now you are Light in the Lord; walk as children of Light.* (Eph. 5:3–8)

Paul left no doubt that it was impossible for any immoral or impure person or covetous man who is an idolater to inherit the Kingdom of Christ. It doesn't matter if that person believes in Jesus, has been baptized or can speak in tongues. If they become immoral or anything like that, they will not have any inheritance in the Kingdom of Christ and God. He said, let no one deceive you with empty words. Empty words are like telling people that they have eternal life when they have not repented of their sins and are not taking up their cross and have not counted the cost of being a disciple of Jesus Christ.

The vast majority of what is called the gospel today is made up of empty words. To tell someone that they are saved because they prayed a "sinner's prayer" (which is not in the Bible) without telling them to give up their life and to love God with all their heart is an example of more empty words. To tell someone that once they are saved, they are always saved are more empty words that are in contradiction to the Bible. There are many empty words that are used today to deceive people into believing they have eternal life. But few find life, because few find the truth and few bear their own cross.

> *Or do you not know that the unrighteous will not inherit the kingdom of God? Do not be deceived; neither fornicators, nor idolaters, nor adulterers, nor effeminate, nor homosexuals, nor thieves, nor the covetous, nor drunkards, nor revilers, nor swindlers, will inherit the kingdom of God.*
> (1 Col. 6:9–10)

In this age of sexual revolution, there are many who claim to be "Christian" who are practicing sin, acts of unrighteousness. There are church members committing fornication, adultery, and homosexuality. There are many pastors and priests who are having or have had sexual relations with their church members. There are even some churches that now perform same sex marriages and have homosexual ministers. Not to mention that now in the church there are many other types of sins such as gossip, lust, pornography, un-forgiveness, jealously, pride, anger, dishonesty, etc. I have heard of men, especially young men, that go to church just to lust over the ladies who are dressed immodestly. These are all acts of unrighteousness, and Paul made it clear that those who committed these sins will not inherit the Kingdom of God. Again, Paul shows that the way is narrow because of immorality as well as all other sins.

About 80 percent of Americans claim to be Christian. If these 80 percent were truly born-again, we would not see the practice of sin as we do today in the modern church. And if those professing "Christians" were not practicing sin, they would have hope of eternal life, but since they do practice sin and belong to a church, they are on the broad way which leads to hell forever and ever even though they "worship" God outwardly on the weekend at some church.

John the apostle wrote this concerning those who are born again:

> *Little children, **make sure no one deceives you**; the one who practices righteousness is righteous, just as He is righteous; **the one who practices sin is of the devil**; for the devil has sinned from the beginning. The Son of God appeared for this purpose, to destroy the works of the devil. No one who is born of God practices sin, because His seed abides in him; and he cannot sin, because he is born of God. By this the children of God and the children of the devil are obvious: **anyone who does not practice righteousness is not of God, nor the one who does not love his brother**.* (1 John 3:7–10)

Again, make sure that no one deceives you. He would not have written this if there wasn't a danger that you could be deceived. Today the modern belief is that everyone is a sinner (one who practices sin), even the "Christian," even the born again "Christian." It is commonly believed that it is normal for a believer to practice sin. I have even heard pastors support this position by saying, "I am just a poor sinner saved by grace. I sin every day." They contradict the scriptures when they say that because the scriptures say that the one who is born again does not practice (commit) sin, much less sin every day. In fact, the scriptures say that no one who is born of God practices (commits) sin and the clear difference between the child of God and the child of the devil is that the child of God does not practice (commit) sin and the child of the devil does practice (commit) sin. Since this is true, the church and the paid pastors that support the idea that it is normal for Christians to sin, especially all the time, are the children of the devil because they commit sin and excuse sin in the church.

Just for clarity, to practice is to do something repeatedly. If you used to get drunk every day and now you only get drunk once per week, or just once per year, you are still practicing drunkenness. It doesn't matter how often or how few times you do it repeatedly, it is still your practice if you still do it even occasionally. If you repent, you stop doing it at all. I used to practice committing adultery on a regular basis. If I now committed adultery just one time per year, each year, I would still be practicing adultery and would still be under the wrath and judgment of God. Some people compare how much less they practice a certain sin with how much more they used to and somehow justify themselves because they are doing "better" than before. Repentance is not doing better. Repentance is turning away from the sin completely.

Also, I must say that there is a difference between willful sin and unintentional sin. Willful sin is when you go ahead to do something that you know is wrong and you choose to do it anyway. This includes sins like adultery, pornography, stealing, lying, unforgiveness, cheating, pretending and any intentional wrong done to another. Unintentional sin is when you stumble and do something you didn't mean to do, like get angry, say something you shouldn't have without thinking first, doing something in a selfish way, having a lustful moment, having a prideful moment, bragging too much, reacting to criticism, returning insult for insult, etc. All of which are usually emotional reactions to something but were not planned or intentional, but are still considered to be sin. The true believer can sin in this way and does have forgiveness without losing his soul. But if he is a true Christian, he will repent quickly, confess his sins and make it right with all parties involved.

> *__For we all stumble in many ways__. If anyone does not stumble in what he says, he is a perfect man, able to bridle the whole body as well.* (Jas. 3:2)

There is a big difference between stumbling that results in tripping and falling into a mud puddle vs. taking an intentional dive into the mud. It is always about the motive of the heart. God looks at the heart, while man looks on the outside. Be very careful about your motives and the reasons why you do things. You can fool man but not God.

> *My little children, I am writing these things to you* **so that you may not sin**. **And if anyone sins, we have an Advocate with the Father, Jesus Christ the righteous; and He Himself is the propitiation for our sins**; *and not for ours only, but also for those of the whole world. By this we know that we have come to know Him, if we keep His commandments.* **The one who says, "I have come to know Him," and does not keep His commandments, is a liar, and the truth is not in him**; *but whoever keeps His word, in him the love of God has truly been perfected. By this we know that we are in Him:* **the one who says he abides in Him ought himself to walk in the same manner as He walked**. (1 Jn. 2:1–6)

So see here that it is possible for a Christian to stumble and sin. But he wrote "IF" you sin, not as you "continue" to sin. For a Christian, sin should be the rare exception for him, not a normal thing to be expected. As he grows in the grace and knowledge of the Lord, he should leave behind the emotional reactions and fleshly responses to situations that in the past caused him to stumble. John said that he wrote these things "that you may not sin" meaning that you should come to a place where you didn't sin anymore, certainly not intentionally. I must add this in as well. A Christian can also sin intentionally. It does sometimes happen. But God has a remedy for that as well. He will discipline His child who commits sin. Then God will give him time to repent. But if he refuses the correction and does not repent in due time, the Lord will eventually cut him off like a branch without fruit and cast him into the eternal fire. The Lord is patient and longsuffering. No one can ever blame the Lord. Also, the Lord is not some angry God just waiting for us to sin, so He can condemn us. He does not desire the death of anyone, but that everyone would repent and turn to Him for mercy. But just because He is patient and longsuffering, we should not test the Lord and play around with sin because the wages of sin is still death for *anyone* who will continue in wrongdoing.

> *Therefore, brethren,* **_be all the more diligent to make certain about His calling and choosing you_**; *for as long as you practice these things, you will never stumble; for in this way the entrance into the eternal kingdom of our Lord and Savior Jesus Christ* **_will be abundantly supplied to you_**. (2 Pet. 1:10–11)

Here Peter after listing certain qualities we should possess, stated that as long as you practice these things, that you would never stumble and in this way the entrance into the eternal kingdom would be abundantly supplied to you. So again there is no excuse for any of us to continue to live with sin. By practicing the qualities Peter outlined in this chapter, we should not continue indefinitely to stumble in unintentional sins, much less intentional sins. We must be about overcoming even the smallest of sins in our lives.

> *"**He who overcomes will inherit these things, and I will be his God and he will be My son**. "But for the cowardly and unbelieving and abominable and murderers and immoral persons and sorcerers and idolaters and all liars, their part will be in the lake that burns with fire and brimstone, which is the second death."* (Rev. 21:7–8)

There is really no excuse for anyone to continue in sin of any kind. The wages of sin are still death, death of the soul forever and forever. Obviously, only a few will ever overcome sin.

Peter the apostle wrote this concerning the church:

> ***For it is time for judgment to begin with the household of God***; *and if it begins with us first, what will be the outcome for those who do not obey the gospel of God?* ***AND IF IT IS WITH DIFFICULTY THAT THE RIGHTEOUS IS SAVED, WHAT WILL BECOME OF THE GODLESS MAN AND THE SINNER?*** *Therefore, those also who suffer according to the will of God shall entrust their souls to a faithful Creator in doing what is right.* (1 Pet. 4:17–19)

Why would there be judgment beginning with the household of God if it was pure? And if it begins first with the people of God, what will be the outcome of those who don't obey the gospel? What does the gospel require, but to take up your cross, deny yourself of sin and worldly pleasures, live obedient to God and love Him with all your heart? Does the gospel of Jesus not require that you give up your life and accept the rejection of family and friends in order to receive eternal life? So what is the outcome of those who don't obey the gospel of Jesus? If it is with difficulty that the righteous is saved (it is difficult because of the narrow way), what will become of the godless man (the religious church goer who practices sin) and the sinner (who makes no claim to God)? Peter then goes on to say that those who suffer according to the will of God (on their cross) shall entrust their souls to a faithful Creator (Jesus) in doing what is right.

> ***"For the gate is small and the way is narrow that leads to life, and there are few who find it."*** (Matt. 7:14)

Remember there are only a few, not many, who are being saved.

> *"For the coming of the Son of Man **will be just like the days of Noah**. "For as in those days before the flood they were eating and drinking, marrying and giving in marriage, until the day that Noah entered the ark, and they did not understand until the flood came and took them all away; **so, will the coming of the Son of Man be**."* (Matt. 24:37–39)

In the case of the destruction of the whole world the first time, only eight were saved. Why did Jesus compare His next coming with the days of Noah if many would be saved this time? There were so few saved compared to the millions who were destroyed during the flood. He said that His coming will be just like in the days of Noah, when only eight souls were saved. Compared to the billions today, I wonder how few will really be saved.

So it is a heart issue. Only the one who loves God with all his heart will be saved.

> *For he is not a Jew who is one outwardly, nor is circumcision that which is outward in the flesh. **But he is a Jew who is one inwardly; and circumcision is that which is of the heart**, by the Spirit, not by the letter; and his praise is not from men, but from God.* (Rom. 2:28–29)

Again, this principle tells us that it is not what you do outwardly in religious service that is acceptable to God, but what you do inwardly from the heart by the Spirit. Few people who claim to know God have their hearts circumcised by the Spirit, but have substituted outward worship for the true worship. Therefore, very few will enter into His kingdom rather than many as most think.

> *And Isaiah cries out concerning Israel, "THOUGH THE NUMBER OF THE SONS OF ISRAEL BE AS THE SAND OF THE SEA, IT IS **THE***

*REMNANT THAT WILL BE SAVED; FOR
THE LORD WILL EXECUTE HIS WORD
UPON THE EARTH, THOROUGHLY AND
QUICKLY." And just as Isaiah foretold, "EXCEPT
THE LORD OF SABAOTH HAD LEFT TO US A
POSTERITY, WE WOULD HAVE BECOME AS
SODOM, AND WOULD HAVE RESEMBLED
GOMORRAH."* (Rom. 9:27–29)

Here, Paul is making it clear that even though Israel was the people of God and large in number like the sands of the sea, that only a remnant (small number leftover) would be saved. It has always been that way and is no different today. Even though the number of so-called Christians are as the sand of the sea, only a few will be saved. So are you on the narrow path or the broad way? Do you worship the Lord in vain or do you worship Him in Spirit and truth? Do you have the fear of the Lord to keep you from sin or do you have a false peace that you can practice sin as a believer? Do you seek God for life or did you settle with the "sinner's prayer" as a method of finding Him? Do you hunger and thirst for righteousness? Do you want the truth or would you rather have your ears tickled?

So is the idea that many or most will be saved, a biblical *truth* or a *myth*?

Chapter 6

The Myth of Grace vs. Works

> *For by grace you have been saved through faith; and that not of yourselves, it is the gift of God; not as a result of works, so that no one may boast.*
>
> —Ephesians 2:8–9

There are two kinds of works in the Bible.

1. Works of the law (religious works, good deeds, missions, church programs, rituals, ceremonies, etc.) that will not save you.
2. Works of obedience (obeying God and His Word). Without these works of obedience to God and His Word, you cannot be saved.

Most grace teachers do not distinguish between these two kinds of works (works of the law vs. works of obedience) and teach that any effort on your part to be saved is wrong and that Jesus did everything for you. They teach that any kind of works or effort on your part will not affect your salvation, but only belief or faith in Jesus will save you. I have even heard one preacher on TV go so far as to say that to repent or even forgive others is not necessary for salvation, but only to accept Jesus and believe in Him. He suggested that for you to do something, even do anything such as repentance or forgiveness, in order to be saved was nothing more than an attempt at "works" for salvation.

The Works of the Law

> *Now we know that whatever the Law says, it speaks to those who are under the Law, so that every mouth may be closed and all the world may become accountable to God; **because by the works of the Law no flesh will be justified in His sight**; for through the Law comes the knowledge of sin. Where then is boasting? It is excluded. By what kind of law? Of works? No, but by a law of faith. For we maintain that a man is justified by faith apart from works of the Law.* (Romans 3:19–20, 27–28)

The works of the law is referring to all the religious ceremonies that were required of the Jews: having to go to the temple to worship, having to keep the sabbath, having to only eat certain foods, making various sacrifices, paying tithes, being circumcised, keeping Passovers, observing many rituals, keeping many laws, observing certain religious holidays and following the Jewish traditions.

Today this same pattern is repeated in modern Christianity. Some still keep the sabbath while most go to a "temple" (church building) to worship. Most think that service to God is church attendance. Most still pay tithes. Most still think that there is a certain "Lords" day. There are many, many "Christian" rituals being practiced and most observe certain religious holidays like Christmas and Easter and there are countless other religious traditions that are also being observed.

> *But now that you have come to know God, or rather to be known by God, how is it that you turn back again to the weak and worthless elemental things,*

to which you desire to be enslaved all over again?
You observe days and months and seasons and
years*. I fear for you, that perhaps I have labored*
over you in vain. (Gal. 4:9–11)

This practice of religious rituals and traditions are the works of the Law by which no one can be saved. You can attend church for a thousand years and be no closer to salvation. You can sing in the choir, teach Sunday school, pass out tracts, go to the mission field, pastor a church, feed the poor, be an usher, play in the band, donate your money, rebuild church buildings, assist in disaster relief programs, participate in every church ritual, serve in every church program, practice every "Christian" tradition known to man and do every kind of good deed and still be no closer to salvation. None of these "works" will save you. This is what Paul the apostle was talking about—*"because by the works of the Law no flesh will be justified in His sight."*

The Works of Obedience

Even though it is a popular teaching today that you have no part in your salvation, don't be deceived into thinking that there is nothing you have to do to be saved. There are many actions (works of obedience) that must be done on your part, so you can be saved.

"For God so loved the world, that He gave His only
*begotten Son, **that whoever believes in Him** shall*
not perish, but have eternal life." (John 3:16)

You must believe. This is something you must do to be saved. No one can do it for you, and God won't do it for you. You must believe in God and His son Jesus and believe His Word. Most of our modern grace teachers stop here and tell you this is all you have to do, but there is more.

"He who believes in the Son has eternal life; but (condition) *he **who does not obey** the Son **will not see life**, but the **wrath of God abides on him**."* (John 3:36)

You must obey. This is something you must do to be saved. No one can do it for you, and God won't do it for you. So just believing is not enough, you must obey God or you won't be saved, otherwise the wrath of God is on you.

*And He (Jesus) said to them, "Thus it is written, that the Christ would suffer and rise again from the dead the third day, and that **repentance for forgiveness of sins** would be proclaimed in His name to all the nations, beginning from Jerusalem.* (Luke 24:46–46)

You must repent. This is something you must do to be saved. No one can do it for you, and God won't do it for you. If you continue to practice sin, you will not be saved, because the only way to be forgiven of sin is to stop practicing the sin.

*"Whenever you stand praying, forgive, if you have anything against anyone, so that your Father who is in heaven will also forgive you your transgressions. **"But if you do not forgive, neither will your Father who is in heaven forgive your transgressions**."* (Mark 11:25–26)

You must forgive. This is something you must do from the heart in order to be forgiven and saved. No one can do it for you, and God won't do it for you. If you refuse to forgive others, no matter how wrong they have done you, you will not be forgiven by God. If you are not forgiven by God, you cannot be saved.

*"I am the true vine, and My Father is the vine-dresser. "**Every branch in Me that does not bear fruit, He takes away**; and every branch that bears fruit, He prunes it so that it may bear more fruit.* (John 15:1–2)

*"I am the vine, you are the branches; he who abides in Me and I in him, he bears much fruit, for apart from Me you can do nothing. "**If anyone does not abide in Me, he is thrown away as a branch and dries up; and they gather them, and cast them into the fire and they are burned**. (John 15:5–6)

Here are two more things you must do to be saved. You must *bear fruit* and *abide* in the Lord to be saved. This is something you must do. No one can do it for you, and God won't do it for you. If you are in Christ (the vine) and you do not bear fruit, He will take you away from Himself and cast you into the fire (hell). It is your responsibility to abide (continue) without falling away and to bear fruit. Fruit is not church attendance, religious works or any of the so-called church services and contributions already mentioned, but fruit is a sacrificed life of obedience to God and holiness. It is a life that is transformed into a new creation that is in the image of Jesus. Fruit is the walk of loving God with all your heart and loving others as yourself. You always have the choice to continue in a relationship with Jesus (connected to the vine), and while connected to the vine, you always have the choice to bear fruit. If you don't continue and bear fruit you will be cast away into the eternal fire, even though you once were in Christ, the vine, as one of His branches.

*"At that time many will fall away and will betray one another and hate one another. "**Many false prophets will arise and will mislead many**. "Because lawlessness is increased, most people's love*

*will grow cold. "**But the one who endures to the end, he will be saved**.* (Matt. 24:10–13)

You must endure to the end. If you don't endure to the end of your life, being faithful to God and obedient to his word, you will not enter heaven. This is something you must do to be saved. No one can do it for you, and God won't do it for you. It is your choice to endure or to not endure. Often people start out sincere and repentant, but after hearing the false message about grace and the false message that they are always going to be a "sinner," they let their guard down and give in to the practice of sin since everybody else in the church accepts this thinking.

*Then Jesus said to His disciples, "**If anyone wishes to come after Me, he must deny himself, and take up his cross and follow Me**.* (Matt. 16:24)

You must deny yourself and take up your cross. You must take up your cross and deny yourself to be saved. No one can do this for you and God won't do it for you. Jesus took up His cross, now you must take up yours. Your cross is your place of suffering rejection, persecution, pain, tribulation and loss of sinful worldly pleasures because of repentance. This is the narrow way that leads to eternal life. This is something you must do, or you can't follow Jesus. Everyone talks about the cross of Jesus, but rarely does anyone point you to your own cross. Your cross of self-denial is required, or you cannot follow Jesus, even though you may attend church every week of your life.

The Way Grace Saves Us through Faith

For the grace of God has appeared, bringing salvation to all men, instructing us to deny ungodliness and worldly desires and to live sensibly, righteously and godly in the present age, looking for the blessed hope and the appearing of the glory of our great God and Savior, Christ Jesus, who gave Himself for us to redeem us from every lawless deed, and to purify for Himself a people for His own possession, zealous for good deeds. (Tit. 2:11–14)

Grace is God's unmerited favor. It is far more than we deserve. It has appeared to all men. It is not some covering of our sin as some have made it out to be, but in fact it is actively instructing us to deny ourselves of sin. Since the wages of sin is death, and for grace to instruct us not to sin by telling us to deny ourselves of ungodliness and worldly desires and to live sensibly and godly in the present age (now, today), it then becomes clear how grace saves us. It saves us by instructing us to turn away from what is going to kill us (sin and selfishness), and to turn toward the One who is going to save us— Jesus—when we obey Him by the instruction sent from His grace to us. Sure, we don't save ourselves, but Jesus will only save us when we give Him our whole heart and obey His grace by faith.

This is the grace of God that instructs us not to sin, not the Baptist grace, nor the Catholic grace nor the Pentecostal grace nor any other man-made grace, but the grace of God. It is the unmerited favor of God to send us His Word and to write the law of God on our hearts to instruct us to turn away from sin and the ways of this world and the false religion of so-called "Christian" works of false worship.

Now faith is the assurance of things hoped for, the conviction of things not seen. For by it the men of old gained approval. By faith we understand that the worlds were prepared by the word of God, so that what is seen was not made out of things which are visible. By faith Abel offered to God a better sacrifice than Cain, through which he obtained the testimony that he was righteous, God testifying about his gifts, and through faith, though he is dead, he still speaks. By faith Enoch was taken up so that he would not see death; AND HE WAS NOT FOUND BECAUSE GOD TOOK HIM UP; for he obtained the witness that before his being taken up he was pleasing to God. ***And without faith it is impossible to please Him, for he who comes to God must believe that He is and that He is a rewarder of those who seek Him.*** *By faith Noah, being warned by God about things not yet seen, in reverence prepared an ark for the salvation of his household, by which he condemned the world, and became an heir of the righteousness which is according to faith. By faith Abraham, when he was called,* ***obeyed by going out to a place*** *which he was to receive for an inheritance; and* ***he went out, not knowing where he was going***. (Heb. 11:1–8)

You must exercise faith. Faith is the action taken by you when you believe. Faith always does something. Abraham believed God and it was counted to him as righteousness because Abraham obeyed God. Abraham did something. That proved his faith. Faith always obeys. Without obedience there is no faith. The works of obedience are the manifestation of faith.

> ***"He who believes in the Son has eternal life; but he who does not obey the Son will not see life, but the wrath of God abides on him."***
> (John 3:36)

To believe in Jesus mentally without obeying Jesus keeps one under the wrath of God. The American church today is filled with people who say they believe in Jesus, yet their lives are virtually no different now than they were before their "conversion." Even though they at one time may have started out very sincere and had a heart felt commitment to God.

__What use is it, my brethren, if someone says he__ __has faith but he has no works__? Can that faith save him? __Even so faith, if it has no works, is dead,__ __being by itself__. But someone may well say, "You have faith and I have works; show me your faith without the works, and __I will show you my faith__ __by my works__." You believe that God is one. You do well; the demons also believe, and shudder. But are you willing to recognize, you foolish fellow, __that__ __faith without works is useless__? (Jas. 2:14, 17–20)

Can faith without works save you? Obviously, the answer is NO. Faith that has no works (of obedience), the kind of faith that does not obey the instructions of God (grace) is worthless. A faith that has no action, no real obedience, no life transformation, no true repentance, no cross, no biblical fruit, no abiding, no overcoming, no serious self-denial, no Christ like character, no wholehearted love of God is a false faith that cannot and will not save him. This faith just has a mental belief in Jesus. Even the devils believe that way and tremble.

__But prove yourselves doers of the word, and__ __not merely hearers who delude themselves.__ (Jas. 1:22)

If you are not a doer of the Word, then you are not of the faith. Again, here is something you must do to be saved—be a doer of the Word. No one can be a doer of the Word for you and God won't do it for you. Millions of people attend church each week who are not doers of the word. They do not seek God nor study His Word to apply it to their lives. Much less obey Him faithfully from the heart.

__"Not everyone who says to Me, 'Lord, Lord,'__ __will enter the kingdom of heaven, but he who__ __does the will__ of My Father who is in heaven will enter. (Matt. 7:21)

Again, you must do something. It is he who DOES the will of God that will be saved. No one can do the will of God for you and He won't do it for you. Just to believe in your mind will not save you. You must do the will of God. His will is for you to overcome sin and the ways of the world and to be conformed into the image of Jesus, His son. This will cost you your old life. All the church attendance in the world will not save you, nor the giving of your money nor the serving of good deeds. Only Jesus can save you, and He has conditions. You must meet these conditions for Him to save you. It is not enough that you accept Jesus, but He must *ACCEPT YOU*. He will not accept you if you do not give up your life completely to Him and follow Him wholeheartedly until the end of your life.

So watch out for the false grace teachers. They are everywhere and in virtually every denomination. They are on TV and many have large ministries and are well thought of by millions of people. Notice what Jesus said about the ministers who are well spoken of:

> "***Woe to you when all men speak well of you***, *for their fathers used to treat the **false prophets** in the same way.* (Luke 6:26)

Watch for teachers who present grace to you as a covering for sin; who tell you that all your sins you commit today and in the future are already forgiven; who leave out repentance of sin for forgiveness of sins; and who leave out your personal cross and self-denial. Watch out for grace teachers who tell you that grace is a covering for your sin while you continue in sin. Watch out for grace teachers who tell you that we are all still sinners saved by grace as though we could continue practicing sin, as if grace excuses sin or covers sin. These men tickle ears and are smooth talkers. These men are wolves in sheep's clothing and they will rob you of your soul if you follow their advice. You cannot continue in willful sin and be saved at the same time.

Beloved, while I was making every effort to write you about our common salvation, I felt the necessity to write to you appealing that you contend earnestly for the faith which was once for all handed down to the saints. ***For certain persons have crept in unnoticed, those who were long beforehand marked out for this condemnation, ungodly persons who turn the grace of our God into licentiousness and deny our only Master and Lord, Jesus Christ****. Now I desire to remind you, though you know all things once for all, that the Lord, after saving a people out of the land of Egypt,* ***subsequently destroyed those who did not believe****.* (Jud. 1:3–5)

You see, these grace teachers have crept in unnoticed. It seems like almost no one has noticed them. They are everywhere and in every denomination and on television and radio every day. They are men like Charles Stanley, John McArthur, Billy Graham, Joyce Meyers, and so many others who turn the grace of our God, the grace that instructs us to not sin, the grace that condemns sin, into licentiousness (license to practice sin) and say you can still go to heaven while you continue in sin. They teach that no matter what you do after you are saved, that you cannot lose your salvation. Even commit murder, adultery, rape children or anything else that is evil. If that is believed, then why would anyone deny themselves? If there is no penalty for sin, then why not sin? This is extremely false and dangerous.

For if we go on sinning willfully *after receiving the knowledge of the truth* (knowing Christ), ***there no longer remains a sacrifice for sins*** (there once was for him), ***but a terrifying expectation of judgment and THE FURY OF A FIRE WHICH WILL CONSUME THE ADVERSARIES****.*

Anyone who has set aside the Law of Moses dies with-out mercy on the testimony of two or three witnesses. **_How much severer punishment do you think he will deserve who has trampled under foot the Son of God, and has regarded as unclean the blood of the covenant by which he was sanc-tified_** (he was cleansed by the blood), *and has insulted the Spirit of grace? For we know Him who said, "VENGEANCE IS MINE, I WILL REPAY."* *And again,* **_"THE LORD WILL JUDGE HIS PEOPLE._**" (Hebrews 10:26–30)

He is obviously not talking about a lost person, but someone who was once saved, who once had received the sacrifice for sins, who once was sanctified by the blood of Jesus and who once belonged to God. He said that He would judge His people; therefore, He was not referring to some lost person in this statement.

The way anyone tramples underfoot the Son of God, regards as unclean His blood and insults the spirit of grace, is to willfully continue in sin after being saved. This person will be destroyed in the same fire as all the other enemies of God. God will judge His people!

So is it clear yet? How are we saved by grace through faith? It is the grace of God that instructs you not to lie, cheat, lust, steal, commit adultery or be a pretender.

It is not good works, nor belonging to a church, nor attending worship service that saves us. It is Jesus who saves us through His grace that tells us how to live above sin and through faith on our part as we obey that instruction. God does His part by sending grace to save us, and we do our part by believing and obeying, which is how faith saves us. We can't do God's part and He won't do our part.

Wolves have crept in unnoticed teaching easy "believism" and false grace that tickles ears and gives people a false hope of being saved. This false teaching takes away any personal responsibility and our own cross. Yet they never mentioned that it is a narrow way and how few will be saved. These false teachers make the way very wide and easy to enter. This is the false way that leads to destruction, and most will go that way.

> *"What Then?* **Shall We Sin Because We Are Not Under Law But Grace? May it Never be***!"*
> (Romans 6:15)

Isn't that exactly what so many "Christians" are doing, willfully sinning and saying they are covered by grace? Is it really the Grace of God that allows one to keep on sinning as a "Christian"? If so, then why did Paul say, may it never be? Why are there countless warnings about God's judgment to the churches, if it was ok to practice (commit) sin as a believer? Why did the apostles waste all that ink writing about those warnings to the churches, if there was no danger? Isn't it possible that God's grace has been changed to deceive today's "Christian"?

> *"**Enter through the narrow gate**; for the gate is wide and the way is broad that leads to destruction, and there are many who enter through it. "**For the gate is small and the way is narrow that leads to life, and there are few who find it**.*
> (Matt. 7:13–14)

Again, here is something you must do. You must enter by the narrow gate or you cannot be saved. No one can do that for you and God won't do it for you. The wide gate and the broad way is what has been made easy by the false grace teachers. It sounds good and very large numbers will go that way and end up in hell. Only very small numbers will be willing to bear their own cross and suffer the cost of discipleship. These are the few who are willing to seek God, obey God, follow Him with all their hearts and endure to the end of their lives faithfully.

And someone said to Him, "Lord, are there just a few who are being saved?" And He said to them, **"Strive to enter through the narrow door; for many, I tell you, will seek to enter and will not be able**. (Luke 13:23–24)

Again, Jesus did not give the same answer as nearly all preachers would today. He did not make it too easy or too wide, but He said to "strive" to enter and that the way that was narrow, and that many will seek to enter and not be able. This is very, very serious! Whenever you hear someone say that there is nothing you have to do to participate in your salvation, run, run as fast as you can, because the devil is speaking to you. He is trying to get you to believe a great lie, so that you will relax and do nothing and end up in hell. You have a great responsibility in your salvation, and God will either save your or reject you based on what YOU BELIEVE AND WHAT YOU DO! God has His part and you have your part. You can't do God's part and He won't do your part for you. His grace is telling to do something, so don't be fooled by the false grace. You must exercise faith by obeying grace.

Which grace do you have, a grace that excuses sin or covers up sin? Maybe you have a grace that forgives all sin even before you have committed it or that takes away your sense of urgency if you do sin. Does your grace extinguish the fear of God or tell you that Jesus did everything for you and that there is nothing you can do to be saved? Is yours a grace that tells you that no matter what you do after you are saved, that you will still be saved? Have you embraced a grace that takes away any personal responsibility to seek God, to obey God, to love God with all of your heart, to overcome sin, to bear good fruit, to endure to the end, to forgive others, to strive to enter by the narrow gate, etc.? If any of these are the grace you have trusted in, then you are in great danger of the eternal hell. I strongly urge you to turn to God with all your heart, repent of your sins and turn away from them, give up your false religion, seek God, obey God, so that you might be saved from His judgment and wrath! His grace, the grace of God really can save you!

So is the modern teaching on grace vs. works, a biblical *truth* or a *myth*?

Chapter 7

The Myth of the Sinner's Prayer

What is the sinner's prayer? Where in the Bible did anyone ever pray a sinner's prayer to be saved? What prophet or apostle ever told anyone to pray a sinner's prayer to be saved? Did Jesus ever tell anyone to just ask Him into their heart and repeat certain words after Him in order to be saved?

So what did Jesus say men had to do in order to be saved?

> *"For God so loved the world, that He gave His only begotten Son, **that whoever believes in Him shall not perish, but have eternal life**. "For God did not send the Son into the world to judge the world, but that the world might be saved through Him. "He who believes in the Son has eternal life; but he who does not obey the Son will not see life, but the wrath of God abides on him.* " (John 3:16–17, 36)

One must believe in Jesus to have eternal life. It is not enough to believe in the fact of the existence of Jesus, and the fact that He is the Son of God, and the fact that He died on the cross for our sins. You must believe Him, not just facts about Him. You must obey Him, and give up your life to Him, turning away from your sin, taking up your cross, and following Him faithfully until the end of your life. James said that the devils believe and tremble. They believe the facts of the truth about Jesus, they know who He is, but they do not obey Him or honor Him as God with their actions. So many today believe the facts about Jesus and think that they have saving faith, but without the believing kind of faith that changes the heart, there is no salvation. In John 3:36, it is clear that mental belief alone will not save you, because if you do not obey Jesus, the wrath of God will remain on you.

> *Then He opened their minds to understand the Scriptures, and He said to them, "Thus it is written, that the Christ would suffer and rise again from the dead the third day, and that **repentance for forgiveness of sins** would be proclaimed in His name to all the nations, beginning from Jerusalem.*
> (Luke 24:45–47)

Here it is clear that without repentance there is no forgiveness of sin. Repentance is the act of turning from committing sin and turning toward God. It is also about changing one's mind regarding sin and to set one's mind to reject all temptation and to obey God from this point on. Repentance is a complete change of direction and mind. The false grace does not change your mindset regarding sin; it just says you are covered when you sin. Without true repentance, there is no forgiveness of sin. So praying a "sinner's prayer" cannot substitute for repentance.

> *"Enter through the narrow gate; for the gate is wide and the way is broad that leads to destruction, and there are many who enter through it. "For the gate is small and the **way is narrow that leads to life**, and there are few who find it.* (Matt. 7:13–14)

Jesus said that it was necessary for one to enter by the narrow way in order to find life. This word narrow in the Greek means a way of suffering, persecution, difficulty, tribulation and rejection. It is the same way Jesus had to walk, and we must choose to walk in his footsteps. He plainly taught that if He was hated, we would be hated as well. Paul also taught that all who desire to live godly in Christ Jesus would be persecuted. Just praying a "sinner's prayer" will not get you hated or persecuted and will not lead you to the narrow way, but repentance, godly living and obedience to God, will take you there. Therefore, the "sinner's prayer" cannot replace the narrow way that leads to life.

> *And a lawyer stood up and put Him to the test, saying, "Teacher, what shall I do to inherit eternal life?" And He said to him, "What is written in the Law? How does it read to you?" And he answered, "YOU SHALL LOVE THE LORD YOUR GOD WITH ALL YOUR HEART, AND WITH ALL YOUR SOUL, AND WITH ALL YOUR STRENGTH, AND WITH ALL YOUR MIND; AND YOUR NEIGHBOR AS YOURSELF." And He said to him, "You have answered correctly;* **DO THIS AND YOU WILL LIVE**.*"* (Luke 10:25–28) (Eternal Life)

Again, Jesus gave a clear condition for one to receive salvation. You must love God with all your heart and your neighbor as yourself. Jesus did not tell the lawyer to just pray a "sinner's prayer" in order to have eternal life, but that his heart had to completely belong to God, and that he should also love his neighbor as himself. This was something the man must do. This is part of what it takes to have eternal life. No so-called "sinner's prayer" can ever take the place of this vital requirement to have eternal life.

> *And someone came to Him and said, "Teacher, what good thing shall I do that I may obtain eternal life?" And He said to him, "Why are you asking Me about what is good? There is only One who is good; but if*

you wish to enter into life, keep the commandments."
Then he *said to Him, "Which ones?" And Jesus
said, "YOU SHALL NOT COMMIT MURDER;
YOU SHALL NOT COMMIT ADULTERY;
YOU SHALL NOT STEAL; YOU SHALL NOT
BEAR FALSE WITNESS; HONOR YOUR
FATHER AND MOTHER; and YOU SHALL
LOVE YOUR NEIGHBOR AS YOURSELF." The
young man *said to Him, "All these things I have
kept; what am I still lacking?" Jesus said to him, "If
you wish to be complete, go and sell your possessions
and give to the poor, and you will have treasure in
heaven; and come, follow Me." But when the young
man heard this statement, he went away grieving;
for he was one who owned much property. And Jesus
said to His disciples, "Truly I say to you, it is hard
for a rich man to enter the kingdom of heaven.
(Matt. 19:16–23)

Why didn't Jesus just lead the rich man in a simple "sinner's prayer" and then tell him he had eternal life? Why did Jesus say that it was so hard for a rich man to be saved if all he had to do was prayer the "sinner's prayer"? That is what the vast majority of today's ministers would have done, just have him pray the "sinner's prayer," and then tell him he was saved. Especially since the man was obviously was a "good" moral person and was also wealthy. He would have been welcomed into virtually any church in America today, and then shortly be given a position of leadership or teaching. He would have been given special treatment because of his financial status. Churches and pastors like to get members who are well off financially. They are much more able to support the pastor's programs and his salary than poor people are. They are often referred to as "big tithers."

And then when the rich church member dies, he would get "preached right into heaven" and the pastor would tell about how great of a man he was and how generously he gave to the "work of God." This scenario has been repeated millions of times all over America during the last hundred years since the "sinner's prayer" was invented and has become the most common way used to determine if someone was ever "saved." The "sinner's prayer" has become the standard of measure rather than repentance and a changed life that bears fruit.

> And someone said to Him, "Lord, are there just a few who are being saved?" And He said to them, "**Strive to enter through the narrow door; for many, I tell you, will seek to enter and will not be able**. (Luke 13:23–24)

Surely todays ministers would have conflict with Jesus here. Surely the way is not that narrow or that difficult to attain, is it? Will you believe Jesus or men? When Jesus said just a few, He meant a very small number would be saved. When He said *many* would seek but not be able to enter, He was referring to a very large number, like multitudes being lost. When He said to strive, he meant there would be a struggle to enter by the narrow way, and that most people would want an easier way and therefore would not make it in. That is why the "sinner's prayer" was invented by Satan, to give men a quick and easy way to be "saved" so they could bypass the difficult and narrow way. This false hope has caused millions to be lost.

> "I am the vine, you are the branches; he who abides in Me and I in him, he bears much fruit, for apart from Me you can do nothing. "If anyone does not abide in Me, he is thrown away as a branch and dries up; and they gather them, and cast them into the fire and they are burned." (John 15:5–6)

Jesus did not say if anyone does not pray the "sinner's prayer" he is thrown away and burned up. He said that if anyone does not abide in Him, does not continue in Him, does not bear fruit, does not endure with Him, that he is thrown away, dries up and is burned. That burning is called hell, the fire of hell. Praying a "sinner's prayer" will not keep you out of hell if you don't bear fruit. But if you repent of sin, abide in Christ and bear fruit, you won't need to pray a "sinner's prayer," because you have done what is required to be saved.

> *"At that time many will fall away and will betray one another and hate one another. "Many false prophets will arise and will mislead many. "Because lawlessness is increased, most people's love will grow cold. "__But the one who endures to the end, he will be saved__.* (Matt. 24:10–13)

Again, Jesus did not say that the one who prayed the "sinner's prayer" would be saved, but that the one who endured to the end would be saved. Just like in John 15, you must be faithful to the end and never fall away, no matter what happens in your life. Praying a "sinner's prayer" can never substitute for repentance from sin and a faithful life of obedience to God until the end of your life. Jesus never spoke of a "sinner's prayer" and never asked anyone to pray one, nor did anyone else in the Scriptures.

Jesus taught that we were to make disciples of men, not give them a quick and easy "sinner's prayer" and then tell them that they are saved. This is greatly misleading and will usually lead a person to hell by giving them a false sense of security.

Again, the teachings and traditions of men have replaced the Word of God and the truth.

From ancient times, the Scriptures instructed men everywhere to seek God earnestly in order to find Him. Men were told to be broken for their sins and to come to the Lord in humility and to seek Him in repentance and brokenness, in order to find Him and be saved. This practice was mostly followed until the late 1800s. Before that time, men who preached the gospel normally never told a seeker that he was saved but told the seeker to earnestly seek God until he was reborn by the power of the Holy Spirit. It was always understood that that process could take some time. It could be rather quick or may take hours, days or even weeks. But Billy Sunday (early 1900s) changed all this and reduced this very important time of repentance and seeking God into "just come forward and shake his hand" and he then told whoever did this that they were saved.

Billy Sunday had a referral card with a printed commitment that was to be signed by the "new convert" and sent to a pastor for follow up. This printed commitment on the referral card was later taken and made into the first "sinner's prayer." So after this, when people came forward to receive Jesus, they were taken into a room for counseling to see if they were really sincere. If the counselor decided they were really sincere, they were led in a simple "sinner's prayer" and told that they were saved and born again. Other ministers began to use this method more and more during the early 1900s because it shortened the salvation process from seeking God with repentance in order to find Him, into a quick and easy salvation method to save preachers a lot of time and effort, so they could make "instant" converts. In the 1950s Billy Graham continued with this method and had people come forward to receive Jesus and would have them go into rooms with counselors and be led in a "sinner's prayer."

But as the crowds grew in number, Billy Graham eliminated the counseling process and gathered the crowds up front and then Billy Graham himself prayed the "sinner's prayer" for the masses and then told them that they all were saved and that they had eternal life. As a result of this, there was no longer any counseling, nor follow up and no discipling of the "new converts." It has been reported that most all of those "converts" fell away and never amounted to anything. Yet most of them probably thought they were going to heaven, because men like Billy Graham told them they were saved and had eternal life, even though virtually none of the biblical requirements were met.

We are told by many preachers and teachers today that Jesus has done everything for you and that you don't have to do anything to be saved, except just believe in and accept Jesus. But I ask you again, is that what the Scriptures say?

> *"Not everyone who says to Me, 'Lord, Lord* (just praying words)*,' will enter the kingdom of heaven, but he who does the will* (obedience to God) *of My Father who is in heaven will enter.* (Matt. 7:21)

So what is His will—-to pray a sinner's prayer? Again, Scripture vs. the traditions and teachings of men.

> *And a lawyer stood up and put Him to the test, saying, "Teacher, what shall I do to inherit eternal life?" And He said to him, "What is written in the Law? How does it read **to you?" And he answered, "YOU SHALL LOVE THE LORD YOUR GOD WITH ALL YOUR HEART, AND WITH ALL YOUR SOUL, AND WITH ALL YOUR STRENGTH, AND WITH ALL YOUR MIND; AND YOUR NEIGHBOR AS YOURSELF." And He said to him, "You have answered correctly; DO THIS AND YOU WILL LIVE."*** (Luke 10:25–28)

Here is something that must be done by the person to receive eternal life: he must love God with all his heart and love his neighbor as himself. You see, this is about a total heart change, a transformation, a regeneration, a new person at heart, not just an outwardly change.

The "sinner's prayer" method of salvation is a great falsehood and responsible for the loss of countless souls because it gives a false sense of security and a false belief that one has done what is required of God to be saved. This is extremely sad and dangerous. If you have led someone in the "sinner's prayer" and told them that they were saved as a result of this, then I implore you to go quickly back to that person and plead with them to forgive you and tell them that they must seek God, repent of their sins and follow Him faithfully until the end of their life. Otherwise they will not be saved. And tell everyone you know to stop this horrible method and explain to them the truth about salvation. May the Lord be with you in this. For now, it will make more sense to you, if you will receive the truth, that you will discover what Jesus meant when He said you would be persecuted and hated for His name sake if you do what is right! Because the "sinner's prayer" has become a religious idol and so-called Christian people will hate you if you touch their "golden calf," the "sinner's prayer."

So judge for yourself; is the "sinner's prayer" a biblical *truth* or a *myth*?

Chapter 8

The Myth of Eternal Security

Let me start out by saying that there is security for a believer in his salvation. But that security is conditional, not unconditional as is mostly taught today. Often in the Scriptures a promise is preceded or followed by an "if" or a "but" or the condition to receive the promise is discovered by further study. A statement in the Scriptures that is taken by itself and not considered in the light of other Scriptures might lead many to conclude that the promise has no conditions when in fact it does in view of the rest of the Bible. So it is important to not just pick and choose verses that please the reader, but to take the whole council of God to get the true and complete picture concerning salvation.

A common belief in salvation today is called "once saved, always saved." The belief is that once someone has been saved nothing can be done either by an outside force or by the person himself to cause him to lose his salvation. Some Scriptures, taken alone, seem to support this belief, while many other Scriptures completely contradict this belief. So it is evident that many, many preachers and Bible teachers today are focusing on a few Scriptures favorable to the doctrine, since it is popular, while completely ignoring the many, many other Scriptures that contradict the belief of "once saved, always saved." Any time someone picks out a few Scriptures to support their own view, they have opened themselves up for deception and error. This practice is the recipe for heresy and all false doctrines. This is the very reason we have so many denominations and different "ways to heaven" being preached today.

Here is one simple way to do a truth test. Ask yourself if there are any exceptions to what you believe to be absolutely true concerning your doctrines in the Bible. For example, if someone started a doctrine that stated that "all the sheep in Texas were white." This might seem true if you only looked at the sheep in your part of Texas and they all were white. But if you diligently searched all over Texas and found only one black sheep, then the doctrine of "only white sheep," would be false. It just takes one exception for a doctrine to be false. We are to search all of the Scriptures to get the whole truth, so that we are sure that we know and understand what is really required to be saved.

This is the main thing that matters in life, to find God and the way to eternal life. Approximately 98 percent of American Christians never study the Bible to find out anything for themselves, but trust their pastors to tell them that they are saved and will have eternal life. It is amazing to me that just about any one of these people would never buy a piece of real estate without inspecting it first or buy a car without driving it or invest their hard-earned money without making sure the investment was safe. Yet they will entrust their eternal souls to a man called "pastor" or "reverend," without ever inspecting the Bible carefully for themselves, to make sure he is not mistaken or leading them astray. Even though their soul is worth more than the whole world, they don't trouble themselves to study the Bible to be sure about it. This is a recipe for a trip to the broad way that leads to destruction and many go that way.

> *Be diligent to present yourself approved to God as a workman who does not need to be ashamed, accurately handling the word of truth.* (2 Tim. 2:15)

This really is a call to "study" to show yourself approved unto God. So no wonder so few really are going to be saved. Study is a part of the seeking of God in order to find Him and know His will. Since so few really study as a workman to handle accurately the Word of truth and therefore discover the true conditions for salvation, very few will be saved.

> *"Enter through the narrow gate; for the gate is wide and the way is broad that leads to destruction, and there are many who enter through it. **"For the gate is small and the way is narrow that leads to life, and there are few who find it**.* (Matt. 7:13–14)

If this was the only verse in the Bible, it should be enough to convince us that something was wrong with the modern eternal security doctrine. What conditions separate the few from the many? Here, in the Greek, the words narrow and small actually mean difficult, painful, tribulation, trouble, suffering, persecution, etc., and the word few means a very small amount. Neither the 70 million plus Catholics, nor the 33 million plus Baptists nor the 120 million plus other protestants in America now meet the meaning of the word "few," not to mention the countless people who have prayed the "sinner's prayer" in the last one hundred–plus years in America nor the countless people worldwide since the death of Jesus who have fallen into one of these categories. This overwhelming mass of people does not fit with the word "few" who will be saved. Since the many go the broad way of destruction, it is obvious that most of these people did not go through the narrow/small gate that leads to life; otherwise, Jesus would have said that countless people would find life, not just a few.

So let us examine some of the Scriptures and teachings of men that are used to support the "once saved, always saved" doctrine and see if there are any exceptions to them or any conditions required to receive the promise in any other parts of the Scriptures.

*"My sheep hear My voice, and I know them, and they follow Me; and I give eternal life to them, and they will never perish; and no one will snatch them out of My hand. "My Father, who has given them to Me, is greater than all; **and no one is able to snatch them out of the Father's hand**.* (John 10:27–29)

If we stop right here, without further study, it would seem like a solid case has been built that you can never lose your salvation. It seems to be assured unconditionally. It even points out the fact that no one can snatch you out of the father's hand. I grant you that no one is powerful enough to snatch anyone or anything out of the Lord's hand. But that doesn't mean that if you turn away from Him, that being in His hand would be a good thing or a pleasant thing, when His judgment comes upon you.

For if we go on sinning willfully after receiving the knowledge of the truth, there no longer remains a sacrifice for sins, but a certain terrifying expectation of judgment and THE FURY OF A FIRE WHICH WILL CONSUME THE ADVERSARIES. (Heb. 10:26–27)

This is referring to someone who has been saved through the saving knowledge of the truth, and then goes on willfully sinning afterward. The reason most people today return to their sin after being saved, or continue in their sin, is because of the "eternal security" doctrine preached in most churches today, and the use of the "sinners prayer" for salvation. Read on and find out what happens to you while in the hands of God when continuing to sin.

Anyone who has set aside the Law of Moses dies without mercy on the testimony of two or three witnesses. How much severer punishment do you think *he will deserve who has trampled under foot the Son of God, and has regarded as unclean the blood of the covenant by **which he was sanctified**, and has insulted the Spirit of grace? For we know Him who said, "VENGEANCE IS MINE, I WILL REPAY." And again, "THE LORD WILL JUDGE HIS PEOPLE." It is a **terrifying thing to fall into the hands of the living God**.* (Heb. 10:28–31)

You see, under the Law of Moses anyone could be put to death for breaking the law, even for just picking up sticks on the Sabbath. The breaking of the law required an immediate physical death by stoning or some other means. But under the Law of Christ (repentance of sin from the heart), when you break this law by willfully continuing in sin, after being saved, you will receive a much more severe punishment than just a physical stoning to death. This is a spiritual death. Death of the soul, just like Adam and Eve died in the garden even though they continued to be alive physically for a long time afterward.

When God said they would "surely die" if they ate the wrong fruit, they *surely did die* spiritually when they sinned. The punishment for spiritual death is called hell. There is not usually an immediate physical death when a soul dies due to willful sin. Therefore, this death is not as readily noticed as it would be if one was stoned to death. This is where most of the American church is today, walking around dead in their sins but without anyone noticing that they really are dead.

Did you notice that this warning in Hebrews 10 is referring to someone who "*WAS*" sanctified by the blood of Jesus? In the past, this person was once sanctified by the blood of Jesus; therefore, he was once saved. If he continued in sin after being once saved, would he always be saved? Since he continued in sin after being saved, grace did not save him, because grace told him not to continue in sin, but he did anyway. Therefore, he not only trampled underfoot the precious blood of Jesus that was shed to take away his sins, but he also insulted the Spirit of grace by willfully committing sin after being saved.

So now we have this situation, a man who was saved and afterward continuing in willful sin. Now he is trampling underfoot the blood of Jesus, which had previously washed his sins away. And now he is also insulting the Spirit of grace, who instructed him to stop sinning, and then he finds himself in *the hands of God*. Now, no one can snatch him out of the hands of God and since he is in the hands of God, he is falling under the vengeance and judgment of God. There will be many, many people who will wish that they could be snatched out of the hands of God on judgment day but won't be able to escape. God will judge *his people* (once saved people) who continue to willfully sin after being saved, and they will receive a certain, terrifying expectation of judgment and the fury of fire that will consume (eternally) the adversaries of God. So it is obvious that the statement that no one can snatch you out of the hands of God does not mean that you have unconditional eternal security—that is, if you go on sinning willfully. Since the American church today has virtually the same morals as the world, where does that leave the vast majority of the "church" members today?

Another common teaching by men is "once a son, you will always be a son." They say you can't undo the fact that you are God's son and that the Lord would never reject His own son. This suggests, of course, that if you are a son, you have unconditional eternal security.

> *Therefore be imitators of God, as beloved children; and walk in love, just as Christ also loved you and gave Himself up for us, an offering and a sacrifice to God as a fragrant aroma. But immorality or any impurity or greed **must not even be named among you**, as is proper among saints; and there must be no filthiness and silly talk, or coarse jesting, which are not fitting, but rather giving of thanks. For this you **know with certainty**, that no immoral or impure*

*person or covetous man, who is an idolater, **has an inheritance in the kingdom of Christ** and God. **Let no one deceive you with empty words**, for because of these things the wrath of God comes upon the **sons of disobedience**.* (Eph. 5:1–6)

Notice that Paul was addressing the children of God here, not some group of lost people. In fact, if you look at chapter 1, verse 1, Paul writes "to the saints who are in Ephesus." These are sons of God. He warns them to not participate in any kind of immorality, impurity, greed, filthiness, silly talk, or course jesting. He even went on to say to the sons of God, "For this you know with *certainty*, that no immoral or impure person or covetous man, who is an idolater, has an inheritance in the Kingdom of Christ and God."

So he is telling these sons of God that they better not participate in any of these types of sins. He makes it clear that no one (not even one of God's own sons) would inherit the kingdom of God if he did. He went on to warn that, because of these things, the wrath of God comes upon the *sons of disobedience*. So it is clear, that if you are a disobedient son, that the wrath of God will come upon you. If these sons of God had eternal security no matter what they did, then why did Paul write these things to them? So it is obvious that just being a son is not enough to get you to heaven. You must be an obedient son.

Therefore if you have been raised up with Christ, keep seeking the things above, where Christ is, seated at the right hand of God. Set your mind on the things above, not on the things that are on earth. For you have died and your life is hidden with Christ in God. When Christ, who is our life, is revealed, then you also will be revealed with Him in glory. Therefore consider the members of your earthly body as dead to immorality, impurity, passion, evil desire, and greed, which amounts to *idolatry. **<u>For it is because of these things that the wrath of God</u>** will come upon the **<u>sons of disobedience</u>**, and in them you also once walked* (before being saved), *when you were living in them.* (Col. 3:1–7)

Again, here Paul wrote "to the saints and faithful brethren in Christ who are in Colossae." Of course, these are God's sons. They are the faithful sons of God in Colossae. Paul is giving instruction for them to set their minds on things above and not on the earth. He goes on to tell them to consider themselves "dead to immorality, impurity, passion, evil desire, and greed, which amounts to idolatry." Then he warns them that because of these things the wrath of God will come upon the sons of disobedience. Remember, he is speaking to the sons of God, not some group of lost people who are not considered to be sons. He also reminded them that they once walked in this manner before they were saved, and it is obvious that he is warning them to not go back to their former manner of sins or the wrath of God would come upon them. So again being a son of God is not enough in and of itself to get you to heaven. You must continue in repentance and obedience, being a faithful son. Otherwise, you could end up being a son of disobedience and come under the wrath of God.

Most of us have heard of the prodigal son that Jesus told about in Luke chapter 15. He was the son of a wealthy man, but he left his father and went after the world and its pleasures. Even though he was secure, as long as he was in his father's house, he left His father of his own free will, took his inheritance and spent it all on worldly pleasures. After he came to his senses, he remembered his father and knew he would be much better off to return to his father, and so he did in repentance and humility. Jesus told this parable to explain how anyone can leave the Father's house (salvation) of his own free will and become lost and dead again due to sin, even though he was once alive and secure with his Father.

"So he got up and came to his father. But while he was still a long way off, his father saw him and felt compassion for him, and ran and embraced him and kissed him. "And the son said to him, 'Father, I have sinned against heaven and in your sight; I am no longer worthy to be called your son.' "But the father said to his slaves, 'Quickly bring out the best robe and put it on him, and put a ring on his hand and sandals on his feet; and bring the fattened calf, kill it, and let us eat and celebrate; for this son of mine **was dead and has come to life again; he was lost and has been found***.' And they began to celebrate.* (Luke 15:20–24)

As you can read, the son had become dead in his sins. He had to have been alive before since he came to life again. So that means that a son can be alive in the father's house, go back to the world, sin, die, and be lost again. Then if he chooses to return to the Father in repentance, he can be made alive again. This parable told by Jesus proves that after being born again to a new life, being safe in his Father's house, that a son can leave his Father of his own free will and die. No one snatched him out of the Father's hand, but he left on his own free will and the Father didn't stop him.

But this also proves that a son can be made alive *again* through repentance. So you can be a living son or a dead son or a repentant son made alive again. Whether you are a living son or a dead son, depends on your own choices. You are still a son even if you rebel, just a dead son. So again just being a son, in and of itself, does not guarantee that you will end up with eternal life. You will have eternal life only if you remain with the Father. But if you happen to leave the Father, then you can only be saved if you return to the Father in repentance and humility before it is too late.

It is also a popular teaching today that God's love will save us, even if we continue in sin or return to the practice (commission) of sin. That no matter what we do, we will still be in the love of

God and His wrath will never come on us because He loves us so much.

> *Who will separate us from the love of Christ? Will tribulation, or distress, or persecution, or famine, or nakedness, or peril, or sword? Just as it is written, "FOR YOUR SAKE WE ARE BEING PUT TO DEATH ALL DAY LONG; WE WERE CONSIDERED AS SHEEP TO BE SLAUGHTERED." But in all these things we over-whelmingly conquer through Him who loved us. For I am convinced that neither death, nor life, nor angels, nor principalities, nor things present, nor things to come, nor powers, nor height, nor depth, nor any other created thing, will be able to separate us from the love of God, which is in Christ Jesus our Lord.* (Rom. 8:35–39)

The fact that nothing on the earth or in the heavenly realm can separate us from the love of God does not mean that we cannot turn away, fall away or rebel anytime we choose to by our own will. God always gives us the free choice to do as we choose to do. Nothing in heaven or on the earth separated the prodigal son from the love of His father. He did it himself, when he left his father's house. As a result of his leaving, he died spiritually (his soul was dead and lost). And if he had not returned to the father in repentance, he would have remained dead and would have been lost forever.

> *"I love those **who love me**; And those **who dili-gently seek me** will find me."* (Prov. 8:17)

So what about the ones who don't love Him or the ones who don't diligently seek Him? Does He love them as well? Why would the Lord make a statement like this if He loves everybody the same?

> *"I have loved you," says the LORD. But you say, "How have You loved us?" "Was not Esau Jacob's brother?" declares the LORD. "Yet I have **loved Jacob**; but I have **hated Esau**, and I have made his mountains a desolation and appointed his inheritance for the jackals of the wilderness."* (Mal. 1:2–3)

So here we have an exception to God loving everyone at all times. There were two brothers, they both were the sons of Isaac, the son of Abraham. God loved one and hated the other. Why did God hate Esau? Was it not because of his sin and rebellion to God? Why did God love Jacob? Was it not because He loved God enough to wrestle with the Angel of the Lord until he was blessed? Was this not a diligent effort on Jacob's part to seek God?

So how do we know if we love God and if we are loved by God? Surely, we don't want to end up in the same place with God as Esau did, being hated by God, do we?

> *"Just as the Father has loved Me, I have also loved you; **abide in My love**. "**If you keep My commandments, you will abide in My love**; just as I have kept My Father's commandments and abide in His love."* (John 15:9–10)

So here Jesus is instructing us to abide in His love. Abide means to continue in His love. This again is a choice we must make. Why would He tell us to continue in His love if it was unconditional? So what was the condition given for us to continue to be in the love of Jesus? There it is, the condition "IF," you keep his commandments, then and only then will you abide in His love. If you don't, you obviously will be under His wrath. Either He loves you or you are under His wrath. You cannot be in the love of God and under the wrath of God at the same time.

> *"**If you love Me**, you will keep My command-ments."* (John 14:15)

It is clear and simple: if you love God, you will obey God. If you don't obey Him, you don't love Him. And He loves those who love Him. That is, those who obey Him. If He loves those who love and obey Him, then obviously He does not continue to love those who don't continue to seek Him and obey Him.

> *Jesus answered and said to him, "**If anyone loves Me, he will keep My word**; and My Father will love him, and We will come to him and make Our **abode with him**. "**He who does not love Me does not keep My words**; and the word which you hear is not Mine, but the Father's who sent Me.* (John 14:23–24)

So again, it is so plain. God loves and lives in those who obey Him, and does not love and live in those who don't obey Him, even if they were once saved sometime in the past. But if they do not continue to obey Him, they will not always be saved.

If you see someone who says he loves God, yet he does not keep/obey God's word, he is a liar. And rather than being loved by God, he is under the wrath of God.

> *"Those who **hate the LORD would pretend obe-dience** to Him, And their time of **punishment would be forever**."* (Ps. 81:15)

Pretending to obey God by church attendance and doing the so-called worship, in reality, means that you really hate God. Pretending to obey God by participating in religious rituals and praying meaningless repetitions to God means you hate Him. If you truly love and obey God from the heart, none of those other religious things will matter to you or to God.

There is true church fellowship that everyone should seek to belong to. No one should be an island to themselves. The Lord intended for us to be with other believers and not to be alone. Even if it is just one or two of you. See the last paragraph of this chapter for more on this.

So again how do we know that we love God and if He loves us? What do we need to find out in order to know if the love of God or the wrath of God is poured out on us? You can't have the love of God and the wrath of God at the same time. He either loves you or hates you. You are either being saved or being destroyed. And that choice is yours, not His alone.

> *By this we know that we have come to know Him, **if we keep His commandments**. The one who says, "I have come to know Him," and does not keep His commandments, is a liar, and the truth is not in him; but whoever keeps His word, in him the love of God has truly been perfected. By this we know that we are in Him: the one who says he abides in Him ought himself **to walk in the same manner as He walked**.* (1 John 2:3–6)

There are multitudes of "professing Christians" who claim to know Him, but by their very actions of living according to the flesh, they are denying Him. Jesus said that if anyone denies Him before men, that He would deny them before His father in heaven.

> *To the pure, all things are pure; but to those who are defiled and unbelieving, nothing is pure, but both their mind and their conscience are defiled. **They profess to know God**, but by their deeds they deny Him, being detestable and disobedient and worthless for any good deed.* (Tit. 1:15–16)

This is the condition of the modern church today in America. They profess to know God, but by their deeds they deny Him. This is the church that bows down to the god of man-made religion, the god of materialism, the god of immoral sex, the god of worldly entertainment, the god of sports (especially football), the god of sexual perversion, the god of pornography, the god of immodesty, the god of abortion, the god of money, the god of political correctness, the god of pride, the god of self-love, the god of pleasure, the god of passivity and the god of immediate gratification, etc., etc.

Another popular belief today is that the Lord will never leave or forsake his own son no matter what that son does. Somehow it is believed that God will remain faithful to His relationship with us, to save us, even if we are unfaithful to Him.

> *"As for you, my son Solomon, know the God of your father, and serve Him with a whole heart and a willing mind; for the LORD searches all hearts, and understands every intent of the thoughts. If you seek Him, He will let you find Him; **but if you forsake Him, He will reject you forever**."*
> (1 Chron. 28:9)

In this Scripture, David is warning his son Solomon to serve God with a whole heart and willing mind, explaining to him that if Solomon did forsake the Lord that the Lord would reject him forever. This principle has never changed, no matter what your pastor tells you.

> *Now the Spirit of God came on Azariah the son of Oded, and he went out to meet Asa and said to him, "Listen to me, Asa, and all Judah and Benjamin: **the LORD is with you when you are with Him**. And if you seek Him, He will let you find Him; **but if you forsake Him, He will forsake you**.*
> (2 Chron. 15:1, 2)

Again, here are more exceptions. The Lord is with you when you are with Him. So obviously He is not with you when you are not with Him. And if you forsake Him, He will forsake you. This is why Jesus told us to abide in Him, meaning don't ever leave Him or you won't have Him anymore. These are simple truths and are eternal principles that have never changed. Men have changed them for their own gain and to have something to tickle ears with.

So back to the question. Can a saved person lose his salvation?

> *"Say to them, 'As I live!' declares the Lord GOD, 'I take no pleasure in the death of the wicked, but rather that the wicked turn from his way and live. Turn back, turn back from your evil ways! Why then will you die, O house of Israel?' "And you, son of man, say to your fellow citizens, 'The righteousness of a righteous man will not deliver him in the day of his transgression, and as for the wickedness of the wicked, he will not stumble because of it in the day when he turns from his wickedness; whereas a righteous man will not be able to live by his righteousness on the day when he commits sin.' "**When I say to the righteous he will surely live, and he so trusts in his righteousness that he commits iniquity, none of his righteous deeds will be remembered; but in that same iniquity of his which he has committed he will die**. "But when I say to the wicked, 'You will surely die,' and he turns from his sin and practices justice and righteousness, if a wicked man restores a pledge, pays back what he has taken by robbery, walks by the statutes which ensure life without committing iniquity, he shall surely live; he shall not die. "None of his sins that he has committed will be remembered against him. He has practiced justice and righteousness; he shall surely live.* (Ezek. 33:11–16)

Here again, the Lord is speaking to His own people. The principle is this, When God tells the righteous (saved person) that he will surely live, and if that saved man so trust in his righteousness (his salvation) that he compromises his righteousness and commits sin, none of his righteous deeds will be remembered, and in his iniquity, he will surely die. On the other hand, if God tells a man who is lost that he will surely die, and he turns from his sin and repents and obeys God by doing what is right, then he will surely live. This is the same theme throughout the entire Bible.

It is really the simplicity of the Gospel. Anytime anyone turns from sin and obeys God, he will surely live, if he continues on that path. Anytime anyone who is righteous (saved) turns from the right path and falls away from God and willfully begins to sin, he will surely die (lose his soul), unless he repents and returns to the Lord and endures to the end. The saved person can be lost, and the lost person can be saved, and the person who was saved, can be lost again and can be brought back to life when he repents.

*"I am the true vine, and My Father is the vinedresser. "**Every branch in Me that does not bear fruit, He takes away**; and every branch that bears fruit, He prunes it so that it may bear more fruit. "You are already clean because of the word which I have spoken to you. "**Abide in Me**, and I in you. As the branch cannot bear fruit of itself unless it abides in the vine, so neither can you unless you abide in Me. "I am the vine, you are the branches; he who abides in Me and I in him, he bears much fruit, **for apart from Me you can do nothing**. "**If anyone does not abide in Me, he is thrown away** as a branch and dries up; and they gather them, **and cast them into the fire and they are burned**. "If you abide in Me, and My words abide in you, ask whatever you wish, and it will be done for you.* (John 15:1–7)

Again, the condition of life for the one in Christ (the vine) is to abide, to continue without falling away. Notice all the "Ifs," the conditions of the promises concerning bearing fruit, having prayers answered and salvation. It is all conditional upon one's own choices.

> But the Spirit explicitly says that in later times **some will fall away from the faith**, paying attention to **deceitful spirits and doctrines of demons** (1 Tim. 4:1).

You cannot fall away from something if you didn't have it. This again shows that salvation is conditional.

Jesus said that every branch in Him that does not bear fruit is taken away. No one could be in Jesus Christ unless he had once been saved. So the branch in Christ will not remain in Christ unless it meets the conditions of bearing fruit. So the person (branch) in Christ (vine), who was once saved, which is how he got in Christ, will not always be saved if he does not abide and bear fruit. To bear fruit is to obey Jesus and keep His commandments, and all of His commandments tell us *not* to willfully commit sin and to walk in a manner worthy of Him. Here in John 15, not only will anyone not be able to remain in the vine (Jesus) if they do not bear fruit, but He (Jesus) will take that person (branch) away (cut off) and cast them into the fire and burn them. This fire is called hell and it is for eternity.

> Or do you not know that the unrighteous will not inherit the kingdom of God? **Do not be deceived**; neither fornicators, nor idolaters, nor adulterers, nor effeminate, nor homosexuals, nor thieves, nor the covetous, nor drunkards, nor revilers, nor swindlers, will inherit the kingdom of God. (1 Co. 6:9–10)

Here Paul was addressing the church again, not a group of lost people. He was warning the church that they should not be deceived into thinking that they could be unrighteous in their actions and still be saved. There would be no warning to not be deceived if you couldn't be deceived about this. If Paul was here today, I believe that he would go directly to the Baptist church first and then to all the other denominations and tell them the same thing, because all of the denominations are filled with immoral people who are relying on the false doctrine of "once saved, always saved" to deliver them into heaven.

Because of this false doctrine, the church is filled with fornicators, idolaters of many things, covetous, drunkards, homosexuals, adulterers, gossips, pornographers, swindlers in business, lustful and greedy members, bitter unforgiving people, jealous, selfish, prideful, deceitful, and lying members who are hypocrites pretending to belong to God. Even if some of them were once saved, they will not always be saved if they continue to live in sin and do not repent and return to the Lord with all their heart.

> *Now the deeds of the flesh are evident, which are: immorality, impurity, sensuality, idolatry, sorcery, enmities, strife, jealousy, outbursts of anger, disputes, dissensions, factions, envying, drunkenness, carousing, and things like these, of which I forewarn you, just as I have forewarned you, that **those who practice such things will not inherit the kingdom of God**. (Gal. 5:19–21)*

Here in Galatians Paul again warns the church (children of God) that if they practice the deeds of the flesh, that they would not inherit the Kingdom of God. He did not add this common remark of today, "unless you are saved," like I have heard many OSAS teachers say.

> *And someone said to Him, "Lord, **are there just a few who are being saved**?" And He said to them, "**Strive to enter through the narrow door; for***

many, I tell you, will seek to enter and will not be able. *"Once the head of the house gets up and shuts the door, and you begin to stand outside and knock on the door, saying, 'Lord, open up to us!' then He will answer and say to you, 'I do not know where you are from.' "Then you will begin to say, 'We ate and drank in Your presence, and You taught in our streets'; and He will say, 'I tell you, I do not know where you are from; DEPART FROM ME, ALL YOU EVILDOERS.' "In that place there will be weeping and gnashing of teeth when you see Abraham and Isaac and Jacob and all the prophets in the kingdom of God, but yourselves being thrown out*. (Luke 13:23–28)

The question was, "Are there just a few being saved?" Jesus said for them to strive to enter by the narrow door and that many will seek to enter but not be able to. This doesn't sound like what is preached today, with the easy "believism" and a sinner's prayer being offered as the quick and easy way to heaven. The Greek word here for *strive* means to struggle, to contend, to fight, to labor fervently, to push, to overcome.

This is why Jesus said if we wanted to follow Him that we should take up our cross and deny self and follow after Him. This is why He said that if you loved Him you would be hated and that your enemies would be members of your own household. This is why Paul said that if anyone desires to live godly in Christ Jesus that he would be persecuted. This is why John, in the book of Revelation said that we must overcome to be with Him. This is why Jesus said that it is the one who endures to the end that will be saved and that the way to life is paved with tribulation, suffering, pain, rejection, persecution, and a cross that you must bear, and that only a few will find this narrow way with a very small gate which is the only way that leads to eternal life.

> *For it is time for* **_judgment to begin with the house-_**
> **_hold of God_**; *and if it begins with us first, what will*
> *be the outcome for those who do not obey the gos-*
> *pel of God? AND IF IT IS WITH DIFFICULTY*
> *THAT THE RIGHTEOUS IS SAVED, WHAT*
> *WILL BECOME OF THE GODLESS MAN*
> *AND THE SINNER?* (1 Pet. 4:17–18)

Judgment begins first with the household of God, and what will the outcome be for those in the household of God who don't obey the gospel of God? And if it is with difficulty that the righteous is saved, then how could anyone be saved with just an easy "sinner's prayer." Beyond the righteous, there are two more categories of people, the godless man and the sinner. The godless man is most likely the church going man who thinks he is saved while he lives a carnal lifestyle. The sinner is most likely the lost man who makes no claim to be a Christian at all. But it is obvious that the righteous is saved through difficulty which is the narrow way, while the godless man and the sinner will both go to hell. With judgment beginning first with the household of God, the godless man (a hypocrite) will be condemned before the sinner of the world is.

So back to the question. Can a saved man lose his salvation?

> *For if, after they have escaped the defilements of*
> *the world by the knowledge of the Lord and Savior*
> *Jesus Christ,* **_they are again entangled in them_**
> **_and are overcome_**, *the last state has become* **_worse_**
> **_for them than the first_**. *For it would be better for*
> *them not to have known the way of righteousness,*
> *than having known it,* **_to turn away from the_**
> **_holy commandment handed on to them_**. *It has*
> *happened to them according to the true proverb, "A*
> *DOG RETURNS TO ITS OWN VOMIT," and,*
> *"A sow,* **_after washing_**, *returns to wallowing in the*
> *mire." (2 Pet. 2:20–22)*

Here is another exception, A person can escape the defilements of the world by coming to know Jesus, repenting of his sin, being cleansed of his sins and then afterward become entangled in them (his sins) all over again. His being overcome by them will result in him being worse off than before he was first saved. The reason he is worse off now is either because his heart has become hardened and there is no longer any conviction of sin to bring him to repentance or he has received a lie in some form of the "once saved, always saved" doctrine preached today. Either way, he is going to die and go to hell after once being saved.

Generally, when that happens today, the modern response is that either he was never saved or that he is just a carnal Christian saved by grace. The reason they say he was never saved was to support the eternal security doctrine because they don't believe a person can once be saved and then be lost again. The reason they say he may be a carnal Christian is because they don't believe anyone can or has to really overcome sin, so it is generally believed that one can sin his way to heaven once he has prayed the "sinner's prayer" and accepted Jesus. But as we can see clearly that neither one of these positions is valid in view of the Scriptures.

Also, in this passage of Scripture, the person who became entangled again in the defilements of the world that he had once escaped from was worse off now than he was before he was saved. He was compared to a dog who returned to eating his own vomit and to a sow that had been washed clean and who now returned to the mire she was wallowing in before washing. So not only did this person lose their salvation, but they were worse off than before they were saved. Today, I see this all the time. People who are wallowing in the mire of sin and who claim to be saved. They have no fear of God and are trusting in a false doctrine and feel safe and secure while they practice sin. As a result, it is nearly impossible to get them to consider that they are in danger. Their latter state is worse than the first state when they knew they were in danger before they turned to the Lord in the beginning. I have said for years, that it is hard to get a "saved" person to be truly saved, because they think they are going to be saved in the end. The doctrine of eternal security has put them to sleep and taken away the fear of God.

> My **brethren**, if any **among you** (brethren) *strays from the truth and one turns him back, let him know that he who turns a sinner from the error of his way will **save his soul from death** and will cover a multitude of sins.* (Jas. 5:19–20)

Okay, again James is talking to brethren. Those who belong to Christ. And he makes it clear that if any among you "brethren" strays from the truth and one turns him back from being a sinner (one who is committing sin), he will save that brother's soul from death and will cover a multitude of sins. So a brother in the Lord who was once saved, can lose his soul again by straying from the truth. And his soul can be saved again when he turns back to the truth.

> *"To the angel of the church in Sardis write: He who has the seven Spirits of God and the seven stars, says this: 'I know your deeds, that you have a name that you are alive, but you are dead. 'Wake up, and strengthen the things that remain, which were about to die; for I have not found your deeds completed in the sight of My God. 'So remember what you have received and heard; and keep it, and repent. Therefore if you do not wake up, I will come like a thief, and you will not know at what hour I will come to you. 'But you have a few people in Sardis who have not soiled their garments; and they will walk with Me in white, for they are worthy. 'He who overcomes will thus be clothed in white garments; and **I will not erase his name from the book of life**, and I will confess his name before My Father and before His angels. 'He who*

has an ear, let him hear what the Spirit says to the churches.' (Rev. 3:1–6)

Here, Jesus is speaking to the church again. He is warning His church to "wake up." He said their deeds were not completed in His sight. Why would He say that if all they had to do was believe in Him and pray a "sinner's prayer"? Jesus told the church to repent and to wake up or He would come like a thief and they would not know when He was coming. Do you really think He was coming as a thief to take them all to heaven? Only a few had not soiled their garments with sin and they were found worthy of life. He goes on to say that he who overcomes will be clothed in white and He will *not erase* their name from the book of life.

Why did Jesus say that He would not erase their names from the book of life if it wasn't an option for Him. And why would He say that if "once saved, always saved" was a true doctrine? No one could have their name in the book of life unless he had been saved once before. Now, Jesus is revealing that He has an option to erase someone's name from the book of life if he doesn't repent. And now we have a situation where Jesus will erase that once saved person's name if he doesn't repent of and overcome sin. Obviously, Jesus doesn't make idle threats. If He said He will not erase one's name from the book of life when he repents and overcomes, then He must also mean that He *will erase* the names of those who don't repent and overcome. This is certainly a *major exception* to the eternal security doctrine.

> *"At that time many will fall away and will betray one another and will hate one another. "Many false prophets will arise and will mislead many. "Because lawlessness is increased, most people's love will grow cold. "But the one **who endures to the end, he will be saved**.* (Matt. 24:10–13)

You see again, another exception, that you must endure to the end to be saved. It is not enough to just get started with the Lord. You must endure and overcome. We are finally completely saved at the end of our life if we have been found faithful until the end. But if we fall away or turn away from the truth and again get entangled in our former sins, we will be cast out of the Kingdom of God and our name will be erased from the book of life.

Another common statement made today is, "I am just a sinner saved by grace." Often the statement is expanded to say, "And I sin every day. Thank God that I am saved by grace." There is also an idea promoted often that the only difference between a Christian and a lost person is salvation by grace. What is being acknowledged here is that the conduct and the presence of sin is virtually the same in both the "Christian" and the lost person of the world.

> *Everyone who practices sin also practices lawless-ness; and sin is lawlessness. And you know that He appeared in order to take away sins; and in Him there is no sin.* (1 John 3:4–5)

So it obviously everyone who practices sin also practices law-lessness. It is also obvious that they have not understood repentance if they are still sinning every day. And if they are still living a life of practicing sin, then Jesus has not taken their sins away.

> ***No one who abides in Him sins****; no one who sins has seen Him or knows Him. Little children, **let no one deceive you***; *the one who practices righteousness is righteous, just as He is righteous;* ***the one who practices sin is of the devil****; for the devil has sinned from the beginning. The Son of God appeared for this purpose, that He might destroy the works of the devil.* ***No one who is born of God practices sin****, because His seed abides in him; and he cannot sin, because he is born of God. By this the*

children of God and the children of the devil are
obvious: anyone who does not practice righteousness
is not of God, nor the one who does not love his
brother. (1 John 3:6–10)

Again, he warns, "Let no one deceive you." The one who sins does not know God and is of the devil. The one who practices righteousness (doing what is right) is righteous. No one born of God practices sin. So if you hear someone claiming to be a sinner (one who commits sin) saved by grace, then you know he does not know God and is really of the devil. Grace has appeared bringing salvation to all men, instructing all men to deny all ungodliness and worldly desires and to live sensible, righteous, and godly lives. If anyone still sins every day, he obviously did not receive the grace of God and is not born again.

You see, un-regenerated people do not have the power to overcome sin, because they do not have the Holy Spirit. They don't really believe in living a life free from the power of sin. They may have a Baptist spirit or a Catholic spirit or a Pentecostal spirit or some other religious spirit, but not the Spirit of the Living God who takes away sin. That Spirit, the Holy Spirit gives power to overcome to those who come to Him with a whole heart and completely give their life up to Him.

The original concept of "once saved, always saved" was first introduced in the Garden of Eden a long time ago by Satan himself. Even though it was not taught or believed by the early church for 1,500 years, it was reintroduced to the church world by John Calvin in the 1500s and has grown in great popularity in the last two hundred years, especially in the last one hundred years.

Now the serpent was more crafty than any beast of
the field which the LORD God had made. And he
said to the woman, "Indeed, has God said, 'You
shall not eat from any tree of the garden'?" And the
woman said to the serpent, "From the fruit of the

*trees of the garden we may eat; but from the fruit of the tree which is in the middle of the garden, God has said, 'You shall not eat from it or touch it, lest you die.'" And the serpent said to the woman, "**You surely shall not die**!* (Gen. 3:1–4)

You see, God had already told Adam not to eat of the tree of the knowledge of good and evil or he would surely die. At that point in time, Adam and Eve were perfectly secure in their salvation and relationship with God. As long as they obeyed God, they were secure. They could have continued in that place of security in the garden, walking with God indefinitely. As long as they continued in obedience, they were secure. But as soon as Satan convinced them that they "surely would not die," they disobeyed and died. It was a spiritual death of their souls. Their salvation was conditional upon continual obedience because God said that if they disobeyed, that they would surely die. And Satan came along as the serpent and contradicted what God said by saying that they surely would not die. So we have these two doctrines for the believer. The doctrine of God that says you surely shall die if you choose to sin and the doctrine of Satan that says you surely shall not die if you choose to sin. The once saved, always saved doctrine is the doctrine of Satan because it says you surely shall not die after God said you surely shall die if you willfully commit sin after being saved. And every preacher, pastor, evangelist, prophet, or teacher that tells you that you can still go to heaven if you continue in sin is of Satan and you should run from them as fast as you can.

The "once saved, always saved" doctrine is the *MOST DEADLY* doctrine of all time. Untold numbers of people have ended up in hell thinking that they were safe while practicing sin. Satan has used countless preachers for hundreds of years to tickle ears and tell people that they were safe using one form or another of the doctrine, "you surely shall not die."

*Thus says the LORD of hosts, "**Do not listen to the words of the prophets** who are prophesying to you. They are leading you into futility; They speak a vision of their own imagination, Not from the mouth of the LORD. "They keep saying to those who despise Me, 'The LORD has said, "**You will have peace**"'; And as for everyone who walks in the stubbornness of his own heart, They say, '**Calamity will not come upon you**.' "But who has stood in the council of the LORD, That he should see and hear His word? Who has given heed to His word and listened?* (Jer 23:16–18)

So it is nothing new. Even thousands of years ago in Jeremiah's day, there were preachers doing the same thing as we have today—telling the people of God that they will have peace and that no calamity could come upon them, even though they walked in the stubbornness of their own hearts. Obviously, these preachers had not stood in the council of the Lord that they should see and hear His Word. Remember, that those who despise the Lord are the ones who pretend obedience to Him while they refuse to obey God and continue in sin. So it is today.

Back to the New Testament:

And if the first piece of dough be holy, the lump is also; and if the root be holy, the branches are too. But if some of the branches were broken off, and you, being a wild olive, were grafted in among them and became partaker with them of the rich root of the olive tree, do not be arrogant toward the branches; but if you are arrogant, remember that it is not you who supports the root, but the root supports you. You will say then, "Branches were broken off so that I might be grafted in." Quite right, they were broken off for their unbelief, but you stand by your faith.

*Do not be conceited, but fear; **for if God did not spare the natural branches, neither will He spare you**. Behold then the **kindness and severity of God**; to those who fell, **severity**, but to you, **God's kindness, if you continue in His kindness; otherwise you also will be cut off**. And they also, if they do not continue in their unbelief, will be grafted in; for God is able to graft them in again. For if you were cut off from what is by nature a wild olive tree, and were grafted contrary to nature into a cultivated olive tree, how much more shall these who are the natural branches be grafted into their own olive tree?* (Rom. 11:16–24)

Again, there is that big IF, another exception. Notice that there are two choices for the believer who was grafted into the rich olive tree (Jesus), either the kindness of God if you continue in His kindness, or the severity of God to be cut off from Him if you don't. His kindness will lead you to heaven and His severity will lead you to hell. It is obvious that this warning is for those who have been grafted into Jesus; therefore, it is those who have once been saved, but will not necessarily always be saved unless they remain.

*For you yourselves know full well that the day of the Lord will come just like a thief in the night. While they are saying, "**Peace and safety!**" then destruction will come upon them suddenly like labor pains upon a woman with child, and **they will not escape**.* (1 Thess. 5:2–3)

Today, about the only message you can find in any church or ministry is "peace and safety." The doctrine of Satan that "all is well" and you surely shall not die if you commit sin, which is the greatest lie of all time and the very deadly doctrine of "once saved, always saved" are all too common in today's church.

I think the point is now made. If I continue to use all the scriptures and expound upon them all, I could make this chapter a "hundred" pages long. But these many scriptures have more than proven that there are many exceptions to the scriptures that appear to give support to the "once saved, always saved" doctrine. Since there are so many exceptions to the doctrine, then the doctrine has to be false and a very dangerous lie. Because it is false, many countless souls have been lost and many more are going to be lost unless they seek God and enter by the narrow way. This is no game, this is forever.

The fear of God is a lost concept. The fear of God has been taken away by the false doctrines of "peace and safety" preached today. The messages of "all is well" and "no calamity will come on you" and "you will have peace" and "Jesus loves everybody" and "all your sins are already forgiven without repentance" and "just pray the sinners prayer" and "just accept Jesus" and "no matter what you do you will go to heaven" and "Jesus did it all for you" and "there is nothing you have to do" and "you are just a sinner saved by grace" and "and you don't really have to obey God, just be willing to" and "once saved, always saved" and "the rapture will take us away from tribulation," all take away the fear of God!

> *"**For the LORD your God is the God of gods and the Lord of lords, the great, the mighty, and the awesome God who does not show partiality nor take a bribe**. "He executes justice for the orphan and the widow, and shows His love for the alien by giving him food and clothing. "So show your love for the alien, for you were aliens in the land of Egypt. "**You shall fear the LORD your God**; you shall serve Him and cling to Him, and you shall swear by His name.* (Deut. 10:17–20)

It was always God's intention for us to fear Him and in doing so be afraid to do anything other than what is right in how we treat other people and how we obey Him.

*Moses said to the people, "Do not be afraid; for God has come in order to test you, and in order that **the fear of Him may remain with you, so that you may not sin**."* (Exod. 20:20)

No one should be afraid to approach God if they are not sinning. So the fear of the Lord will keep you from sinning. To fear the Lord is to know Him and to know that if you turn from Him and His word and commit sin, you will be chastened and disciplined as a son and then if you don't repent you will be rejected and destroyed. The realization of this truth will give you a healthy fear of the Lord and this fear will keep you away from sin. If you don't have this fear to keep you away from sin, you will have no power to keep from giving into sin. Since the wages of sin is death, this is God's design for us to have protection from temptation of sin, by having a healthy fear of Him.

*Transgression speaks to the ungodly within his heart; **There is no fear of God before his eyes**.* (Ps. 36:1)

Without the fear of God, transgression will take over most anyone's heart. We have a modern American "Christian" church today with transgression speaking to the hearts of ungodly members while they falsely worship God. There is no fear of God before their eyes.

The fear of the LORD is the beginning of knowledge; *Fools despise wisdom and instruction.* (Prov. 1:7)

The fear of the Lord is just the beginning of knowledge, not head/brain knowledge, but true knowledge, the knowledge of who God really is and to know and to understand His ways. The fear of the Lord is not the completion of knowledge, only the beginning of it. So if you don't have the fear of the Lord, you really don't know anything, much less know Him. How ridiculous It is for someone to say, "I know the Lord," while they have no fear of Him. To know Him is to fear Him and to not fear Him is to not know Him or understand Him.

> *The secret of the LORD is for those who fear Him, And He will make them know His covenant.* (Ps. 25:14)

You will not understand the covenant of God for His people without the fear of the Lord. The gospel and the salvation plan for man were both established before the foundation of the world and they are a mystery. And that mystery is only revealed to those who fear Him. The rest get the teachings and traditions of men, religious ceremonies, church rituals and various religious superstitions. As a result, they will end up with a false gospel that leads them to hell forever. Only those who seek the Lord with all their heart will ever find Him and the narrow way He will lead them through to find life. It has always been that way between God and man, from the beginning of time. Jesus is the same yesterday, today, and forever.

> *The fear of the LORD is the beginning of wisdom, And the knowledge of the Holy One is understanding.* (Prov. 9:10)

Again, the fear of the Lord is only the beginning of wisdom, not the completion of wisdom. Any preacher or church member who does not have the fear of the Lord has no spiritual wisdom. It does not matter that he may have a doctorate degree in theology or that he has belonged to the church for forty years. Without the fear of the lord, he has no wisdom.

> *"The fear of the LORD is to hate evil; Pride and arrogance and the evil way And the perverted mouth, I hate."* (Prov. 8:13)

Ask yourself this, does the average modern "Christian" church member really hate sin, really hate evil, truly hate what God calls evil? And if you are honest with yourself, you would have to say no. No wonder, how could they hate evil without the fear of the Lord?

*In the fear of the LORD there is strong confidence, And his children will have refuge. **The fear of the LORD is a fountain of life**, That one may avoid the snares of death.* (Prov. 14:26–27)

The strong confidence comes when you are without sin and you know you have refuge in the Lord because you know you are right before Him. The fear of the Lord is a fountain of life because it causes you to avoid the snares of death which is to give in to the temptation to sin.

***The fear of the LORD leads to life**, So that one may sleep satisfied, **untouched by evil**.* (Prov. 19:23)

Again, the life that the fear of the Lord leads to is eternal, because it keeps you from being touched by evil. The way it keeps you from being touched by evil is by having the knowledge that God will do exactly what He says if you choose to sin.

***The angel of the LORD encamps around those who fear Him, And rescues them**.* (Ps. 34:7)

If the angel of the Lord encamps around those who fear the Lord, where does that leave the "Christian" who does not fear the Lord? Jesus spoke to His own disciples and said this:

*"Do not fear those who kill the body but are unable to kill the soul; **but rather fear Him who is able to destroy both soul and body in hell**."* (Matt. 10:28)

The Greek word used here for fear is *phobeo*, which means to fear exceedingly or to have terror on you. Why would Jesus say this to His own disciples, if there was no reason to fear God anymore?

Paul said this to the Corinthian church members:

> *Therefore, knowing the **fear of the Lord**, we persuade men, but we are made manifest to God; and I hope that we are made manifest also in your consciences.* (2 Cor. 5:11)

The Greek word used here for fear is *phobos*, which means to fear exceedingly, to be in terror. What Paul is really saying is this, "knowing the terror of the Lord," we persuade men.

The King James Bible reads it this way:

> *Knowing therefore the **terror of the Lord**, we persuade men; but we are made manifest unto God; and I trust also are made manifest in your consciences.* (2 Cor. 5:11)

As you can see, this kind of fear is much more than just having respect or even reverence for God as is mostly taught today. The idea of really, seriously fearing the Lord has been washed away with the flood of false teachings about who God is and how He deals with those who sin after being saved.

> *So then, my beloved, just as you have always obeyed, not as in my presence only, but now much more in my absence, **work out your salvation with fear and trembling**.* (Phil. 2:12)

In the Greek, it reads like this—work out your salvation being exceedingly fearful, in terror and do so trembling and quaking in fear.

When you have this kind of the fear of the Lord, you will be very motivated to deny yourself of sin as you take up your cross and follow Jesus. As you follow Jesus, you will see that He never leads you into sin, but actually takes you away from sin. How can anyone say they are following the Lord while they involved in sin? This is nonsense!

> *I will bless the LORD at all times; His praise shall continually be in my mouth. My soul will make its boast in the LORD; The humble will hear it and rejoice. O magnify the LORD with me, And let us exalt His name together. I sought the LORD, and He answered me, And delivered me from all my fears. They looked to Him and were radiant, And their faces will never be ashamed. This poor man cried, and the LORD heard him And saved him out of all his troubles.* ___The angel of the LORD encamps around those who fear Him, And rescues them. O taste and see that the LORD is good; How blessed is the man who takes refuge in Him!___ (Ps. 34:1–8)

Please, don't think that I am painting a picture that God is just an angry God waiting and watching for you to sin, so He can do something terrible to you. Oh, taste the Lord and see that He is good and that He would much rather save than destroy anyone.

> *"Say to them, 'As I live!' declares the Lord GOD,* ___'I take no pleasure in the death of the wicked___, *but rather that the wicked* ___turn from his way and live___. *Turn back, turn back from your evil ways!* ___Why then will you die, O house of Israel?'"___ (Ezek. 33:11)

So here is the heart of God. He does not desire the death of the wicked, but would much rather see him turn back from his sins and live. So the Lord is telling all of those who claim to be his people to turn back, turn back from your evil ways, from the ways of the world, from the ways of your false religion, from all your American idols and from the ways that are contrary to the ways of God. This is His grace that saves, does anyone hear or care?

God so desires for His people to turn back that He will be patient and even bring discipline to His own children before He completely rejects His own.

> *You have not yet resisted to the point of shedding blood in your striving against sin; and you have forgotten the exhortation which is addressed to you as sons, "MY SON, DO NOT REGARD LIGHTLY THE DISCIPLINE OF THE LORD, NOR FAINT WHEN YOU ARE REPROVED BY HIM;* ***FOR THOSE WHOM THE LORD LOVES HE DISCIPLINES, AND HE SCOURGES EVERY SON WHOM HE RECEIVES***.*" It is for discipline that you endure;* ***God deals with you as with sons; for what son is there whom his father does not discipline****? But if you are without discipline, of which all have become partakers, then you are illegitimate children and not sons. Furthermore, we had earthly fathers to discipline us, and we respected them;* ***shall we not much rather be subject to the Father of spirits, and live****? For they disciplined us for a short time as seemed best to them, but He disciplines us for our good, so that we may share His holiness. All discipline for the moment seems not to be joyful, but sorrowful; yet to those who have been trained by it,* ***afterward it yields the peaceful fruit of righteousness****. Therefore, strengthen the hands that are weak and the knees that are feeble,*

*and make straight paths for your feet, so that the limb which is lame may not be put out of joint, but rather be healed. **Pursue peace with all men, and the sanctification without which no one will see the Lord.*** (Heb. 12:4–14)

This again shows the heart of God for His own children who are still striving against sin. This shows that He is a loving father who will scourge His own son who does wrong and that He does that for our sanctification without which no one would see the Lord. Often the Lord will send someone who is faithful to correct His own children or to rebuke them for sin, because He is patient and does not desire the death of any of His children. In today's modern church, the children of God are spoiled, undisciplined and left to do as they please. The pastors no longer confront, correct, rebuke or discipline them or even remove the unrepentant sinner from the church. The position that is mostly taken now, is to "live and let live" or "don't judge" or "it is none of my business" or "we all are just poor sinners saved by grace," when any of the members sin.

Today, this is called love, to allow a member to continue in sin without correction or rebuke. But the truth is that it is really hate, since the one who continues in sin will fall under the judgment of God and lose his soul in hell forever if not corrected. Just look at the divorce rate in the church today and tell me who is intervening to stop it? Families being torn apart due to sin and selfishness. Where are the shepherds of God who will not tolerate this disaster of divorce? The children of divorce are scattered to the wind and are easy prey for Satan and his demons. This is just one of the many tragedies present in the modern American church today. Do you see any of this yet? Are you grieved as I am? If so, what are you going to do about it? Can you continue to keep silent? Do you fear man more than God?

***Let the righteous smite me in kindness and reprove me**; It is oil upon the head; Do not let my* *head refuse it, For still my prayer is against their wicked deeds.* (Ps. 141:5)

Better is open rebuke Than love that is concealed. Faithful are the wounds of a friend, But deceitful are the kisses of an enemy. (Prov. 27:5–6)

A true friend will tell you when you have done wrong and will stand strong against your sin. He will correct you, instruct you, and rebuke you if need be. Better are the wounds of a friend than the smooth, buttery talk of your enemies. If you don't have any friends who are seriously concerned if you sin, then you are surrounded by enemies who are going to help you get to hell.

*I wrote you in my letter not to associate with immoral people; I did not at all mean with the immoral people of this world, or with the covetous and swindlers, or with idolaters, for then you would have to go out of the world. But actually, I wrote to you **not to associate with any so-called brother** if he is an immoral person, or covetous, or an idolater, or a reviler, or a drunkard, or a swindler--**not even to eat with such a one**. For what have I to do with judging outsiders? **Do you not judge those who are within the church**? But those who are outside, God judges. **REMOVE THE WICKED MAN FROM AMONG YOURSELVES**.* (1 Cor. 5:9–13)

Here Paul is instructing Christians not to associate with any so-called brother if he was a sinner, not to even eat with such a one. He is also rebuking the Corinthians for not judging a certain church member for living in immorality. Also, Paul points out in this same chapter that a little leaven leavens the whole lump, meaning that a little sin will ruin the whole church. So he said to remove the wicked man from yourselves.

> *My brethren, if any among you strays from the truth and one turns him back, let him know that he who turns a sinner from the error of his way will save his soul from death and will cover a multitude of sins.* (Jas. 5:19–20)

Here again, it is obvious that correction for any brother (believer) in sin or error is necessary to save his soul from death. Even though he was once saved, the fact that he strayed from the truth and became a sinner again, required that someone turned him back again to the truth and doing that would result in saving his soul from death and would cover a multitude of sins.

Jesus said---

> *"For nation will rise against nation, and kingdom against kingdom, and in various places there will be famines and earthquakes. "But all these things are merely the beginning of birth pangs. "Then they will deliver you to tribulation, and will kill you, and you will be hated by all nations because of My name. "At that time many will fall away and will betray one another and hate one another.* *__Many false prophets will arise and will mislead many.__* Mat 27:7-11

It is obvious today that many false prophets/preachers/pastors have arisen and have misled many. Are you going to be one of the misled or remain one of the misled?
Peter warned---

> *But false prophets also arose among the people, just as there will also be false teachers among you, who*

*will **secretly introduce destructive heresies**, even denying the Master who bought them, bringing swift destruction upon themselves. Many will follow their sensuality, and because of them the way of the truth will be maligned; and in their greed they will exploit you with false words; their judgment from long ago is not idle, and their destruction is not asleep.* **2Pe 2:1-3**

The most destructive heresies of all are the ones that cause people to believe that they are saved when they really are not, the ones that cause them to believe that Jesus did everything for them and that they have no responsibility to do anything, the ones that cause them to believe that practicing sin is not dangerous and the ones that cause them to believe that nothing they can do could possibly cause them to lose their salvation. All of these heresies and others like these are extremely dangerous and are the inventions of Satan himself. And the American church is full of all these destructive heresies and they are promoted by the false teachers that are among all of us everywhere today.

So if you don't belong to a church that preaches strong against sin, corrects those in sin, confronts false teachers, confronts false doctrines, confronts false brothers, confronts members who sin, continually warns members about the dangers of sin, rebukes those who get into error, removes those who continue in sin, has a sense of urgency, teaches that the way is narrow and only a few will enter in, then you better run as fast as you can. Run for your life and seek God, cry out in prayer and study of His word to find the truth. Do this like your life depends on it, for it really does. In most cases, church attendance is very dangerous for the soul. Most churches are spreading Calvinism (once saved, always saved) in some form or another as well as other doctrines of demons. There are only two options here, to love and obey God with all your heart or to be lost for all eternity. There is no other option.

So I must tell you that there is security for a believer, but as proven by these many Scriptures, it is a conditional eternal security. You don't have to lie in bed at night wondering if you have any hope or if you are going to hell. As long as you seek God and obey Him, you are secure. It is not about a bunch of religious rules of do's and don'ts, or church attendance, but about a heart that is given completely to Him. It is not that if you happen to stumble and sin that you immediately lose your salvation, but it is about whether or not you turn away from the Word of God and begin to intentionally commit sin and neglect the correction of the Lord.

If you happen to stumble and sin, you have an advocate with the Father, Jesus Christ the Righteous. That is, *IF* by chance you were to commit a sin, not as though you can continue to sin, that you have that advocate. It should be a very strange thing or completely out of character for you to sin, something very unusual if it happened. It is not normal for a true believer to sin, but because of human weakness, and sometimes a lack of maturity and the work of the devil with temptation, it does sometimes happen. That is why you should belong with other true believers, in a true church, so you can be instructed, confronted, corrected and brought back to repentance.

The Lord is patient and long suffering. He will discipline you, correct you and give you some time to repent, but don't test the Lord. Repent quickly and don't continue to repeat the same sin again. This is a test of where your heart is, with God or with your sin. If you embrace the sin and are overcome by it, then you will be rejected by the Lord unless you later repent and return to the Lord. Everyone is responsible for his own walk and relationship with the Lord. Do not depend on your priest or pastor to get you to heaven, but only depend on Jesus to save you. Seek Him continually and obey Him all the days of your life and you will be secure in your salvation.

For the best outcome in your walk with God, try to find true fellowship. Pray and seek for connection with true believers and search for a church that teaches the truths you have seen in the Scriptures so far in this book. Even if you can't find a church like that, try to find one or two true believers. Jesus said that where two or three have gathered together, there He is in their midst. If you can't find anyone, then go out and make disciples of those in your life by sharing the truth with them. Maybe one or two will receive the truth and you will have true fellowship. But remember, there will never be many, only a few who will truly repent and follow the Lord with all their heart. If you never find anyone, don't give up, because the Lord will sustain you even if you are alone with only Him!

So you judge this, is the "once saved, always saved" doctrine a biblical *truth* or a *myth*?

Chapter 9

The Myth of the Rapture

There are various teachings on "rapture" today, but the most popular one says that "Christians" will be taken away first and those who remain will go through great tribulations and troubles here on earth. Since the term "rapture" does not appear in Scripture and since the doctrine of the modern "rapture" has only been around for a couple hundred years, it would be prudent to see what the Bible has to say about it. Pay careful attention to the order in which the end of time unfolds.

> And as He was sitting on the Mount of Olives, the disciples came to Him privately, saying, "Tell us, when will these things be, and what will be the sign of Your coming, and of the end of the age?" And Jesus answered and said to them, "__See to it that no one misleads you.__ (Matt. 24:3, 4)

When Jesus warns, "See to it that no one misleads you," we should pay close attention to what He says after that.

> "__Then they will deliver you to tribulation__, and will kill you, and you will be hated by all nations on account of My name. (Matt. 24:9)

Did you notice that Jesus was telling His own disciples, which includes us, that they were going to be delivered to tribulation and that they would be hated because of His name?

> *"And at that time **many will fall away** and will deliver up one another and hate one another. "But the **one who endures to the end, he shall be saved**.* (Matt. 24:10, 13)

Notice that Jesus did not mention anything about any "rapture" taking them away from tribulation, but that they would have to endure to the end after tribulation to be saved!

> *For then there will be **a great tribulation**, such as has not occurred since the beginning of the world until now, nor ever shall. "And unless those days had been cut short, no life would have been saved; **but for the sake of the elect those days shall be cut short**. "But immediately after the tribulation of those days the sun will be darkened, and the moon will not give its light, and the stars will fall from the sky, and the powers of the heavens will be shaken, and then the sign of the Son of Man will appear in the sky, and then all the tribes of the earth will mourn, and they will see the Son of Man coming on the clouds of the sky with power and great glory." And He will send forth His angels with a great trumpet and they will gather together His elect from the four winds, from one end of the sky to the other.* (Matt. 24:21, 22, 29, 30, 31)

Again, Jesus clearly established here that the saints, His elect, would have to endure all the way to the end, after everything else including the great tribulation had taken place, before they would be taken up to be with Him.

He presented another parable to them, saying, "The kingdom of heaven may be compared to a man who sowed good seed in his field. "But while men were sleeping, his enemy came and sowed tares also among the wheat, and went away. "But when the wheat sprang up and bore grain, then the tares became evident also. "And the slaves of the landowner came and said to him, 'Sir, did you not sow good seed in your field? How then does it have tares?' "And he said to them, 'An enemy has done this!' And the slaves said to him, 'Do you want us, then, to go and gather them up?' "But he said, 'No; lest while you are gathering up the tares, you may root up the wheat with them. 'Allow both to grow together until the harvest; and in the time of the harvest I will say to the reapers, "__First gather up the tares and bind them in bundles to burn them up__; but gather the wheat into my barn."' (Matt. 13:24–30)*

Again, the consistent message is that the tares (lost people, false Christians) will be removed first, bundled for burning, and then the good wheat (true believers) will be gathered to the Lord!

Then He left the multitudes, and went into the house. And His disciples came to Him, saying, "Explain to us the parable of the tares of the field." And He answered and said, "The one who sows the good seed is the Son of Man, and the field is the world; and as for the good seed, these are the sons of the kingdom; and the tares are the sons of the evil one; and the enemy who sowed them is the devil, and the harvest is the end of the age; and the reapers are angels. "Therefore, just as the tares are gathered up and burned with fire, so shall it be at the end of the age. "The Son of Man will send forth His *angels, and **they will gather out of His kingdom all stumbling blocks, and those who commit lawlessness**, and will cast them into the furnace of fire; in that place there shall be weeping and gnashing of teeth. "Then the righteous will shine forth as the sun in the kingdom of their Father. He who has ears, let him hear.* (Matt. 13:36–43)

Again, the sinners and lawless will be gathered out first and cast into the fire, then the righteous will remain to the end and shine forth in His Kingdom! Isn't this contrary to what we have been taught?

*"Again, the kingdom of heaven is like a dragnet cast into the sea, and gathering fish of every kind; and when it was filled, they drew it up on the beach; and they sat down, and gathered the good fish into containers, but the bad they threw away. "So it will be at the end of the age; the angels shall come forth, **and take out the wicked from among the righteous**, and will cast them into the furnace of fire; there shall be weeping and gnashing of teeth. "**Have you understood all these things**?" They said to Him, "Yes."* (Matt. 13:47–51)

So it is not the true Christian who is snatched away first as we have been told, but the wicked who will be snatched away first and thrown into the fire. Again, the true believer has to endure to the end and not fall away in order to be saved!

*"**And just as it happened in the days of Noah**, so it shall be also in the days of the Son of Man: they were eating, they were drinking, they were marrying, they were being given in marriage, until the day that Noah entered the ark, and **the flood came and destroyed them all**.* (Luke 17:26–27)

163

So again, didn't the flood take away all the wicked and leave the righteous? Isn't this the opposite of the modern rapture teaching?

> *"It was the same as happened in the days of Lot: they were eating, they were drinking, they were buying, they were selling, they were planting, they were building; but on the day that Lot went out from Sodom it rained fire and brimstone from heaven and **destroyed them all**. "**It will be just the same on the day that the Son of Man is revealed**.* (Luke 17:28–30)

Again, was it not the wicked who were taken out? Does Jesus not again make it perfectly clear that the first to go will be the wicked? Lot remained but the rest were taken away and destroyed!

> *"I tell you, on that night there will be two men in one bed; **one will be taken**, and the other will be left. "There will be two women grinding at the same place; **one will be taken**, and the other will be left. ["Two men will be in the field; **one will be taken** and the other will be left."]* (Luke 17:34–36)

It is commonly taught concerning these scriptures that the one taken in each of the cases was "raptured" out. Do you see how false that is and how inconsistent it would be with the rest of the scriptures? It has always been that the one taken out first is the sinner who is destroyed! The man taken from bed, the woman taken from grinding and the man taken from the field. These will all be taken away by the reapers that come at the end of the age. They will suffer the same fate as those who perished in the flood and those who burned up with fire and brimstone in Sodom, who are given to us for examples for the end of the age.

It is also commonly taught that we as Christians are not going to suffer any tribulation or trouble and that Jesus did all the suffering for us on His cross. Is that what the Bible says?

*"He who loves father or mother more than Me is not worthy of Me; and he who loves son or daughter more than Me is not worthy of Me. "**And he who does not take his cross and follow after Me** is not worthy of Me. "He who has found his life shall lose it, and he who has lost his life for My sake shall find it.* (Matt. 10:37–39)

Jesus also said,

*"**Enter by the narrow gate**; for the gate is wide, and the way is broad that leads to destruction, and many are those who enter by it. "**For the gate is small, and the way is narrow that leads to life, and few are those who find it**.* (Matt. 7:13–14)

Here in these scriptures we are told that the narrow way and small gate are the only way to life. The Greek meanings of narrow and small here are tribulation, suffering, difficulty, pain, hardship, etc. The false doctrine on rapture says that you will be taken away from the tribulation and that you will not suffer the pain and hardship of this narrow way, but the opposite is true. The narrow way of tribulation, trials, persecutions, rejection, being hated, difficulty and having to endure to the end to be saved is the only way to life. If you don't go through the narrow way, the narrow gate, the way of tribulation, then you will not enter eternal life. It is your cross you must bear and your life you must give up in order to be saved!

*Now as to the times and the epochs, brethren, you have no need of anything to be written to you. For you yourselves know full well that **the day of the Lord will come just like a thief in the night**. While they are saying, "**Peace and safety**!" then destruction will come upon them suddenly like birth pangs upon a woman with child; and **they shall not escape**. But you, brethren, are not in darkness, that the day should overtake you like a thief; for you are all sons of light and sons of day. We are not of night nor of darkness; so then let us not sleep as others do, but let us be alert and sober.* (1 Thess. 5:1–6)

You see, destruction will come suddenly upon those who are saying and believing "Peace and safety"! It is only those who are entering by the narrow (difficulty, tribulation, persecution) way that will be saved. The modern rapture doctrine is another false peace and safety message, similar to the "once saved, always saved" doctrine. We were warned to be sober and be on the alert. In the beginning of this chapter, Jesus said for us to not be deceived. He wouldn't have said to not be deceived if there wasn't a danger that we could be deceived.

So where did the rapture doctrine come from?

It all started with a woman named Margaret MacDonald in 1830. She gave a "prophesy" concerning end times. Her "prophesy" was written down and later published in 1840 and again in 1861. From this "prophesy" a man named John Nelson Darby began to promote the concept of the rapture "theory" and it began to become popular. C. I. Scofield, a well-known theologian of the late 1800s and early 1900s, liked the rapture theory and began to include it in his annotated Bibles, and from there, it became widely popular in most American churches. So this is a new and modern doctrine that was never taught or thought up before 1830. Yet it is taught and believed to be true by almost every denomination and paid preacher we have today. The reason it is so popular is because it is just another way

Satan has to tickle ears, by telling "Christians" that they won't have to suffer and that they will have a way of escape from tribulation.

This "escapism" mentality is just another version of the lie that a Christian does not have to bear a cross and suffer, and it is a part of the easy and broad way that leads to destruction, rather than the narrow and small gate that leads to life. The rapture theory says that you will have no tribulation, but the name of the small gate that leads to life is trouble, tribulation, suffering and pain. No one will enter life without going through the narrow way and small gate of tribulation and bearing his own cross.

You must decide for yourself if the modern rapture doctrine is a biblical *truth* or a *myth*!

Chapter 10

The True Gospel and the True Church

But I am afraid that, as the serpent deceived Eve by his craftiness, your minds will be led astray from the simplicity and purity of devotion to Christ. (2 Col. 11:3)

So what has happened to our modern-day "Christianity" is that the serpent (Satan) has led the minds of our modern church leaders and members away from the simplicity and purity of devotion to Christ by creating all this Christian chaos of many denominations and many ways to heaven with many different "jesuses."

The way to life and heaven is very simple. It is not always easy, but it is always simple. It does include one's own personal cross, persecution, rejection, loss of family and friends, but it is very simple. You don't have to invent your cross or search for persecution and rejection. When you are tempted to sin, there before you is your cross to choose or sin to give into. If you choose to deny yourself of sin, then you will have found your cross.

When you abstain from the worldly practices you once did with your family and they mock you and even reject you because of your love of God, you have found your cross and you are now being introduced to the narrow way. It is very simple, love God, obey God, stand for what is right, turn away from what is wrong, and your cross will be right in front of you, unavoidable and it will take you directly through the narrow way that leads to life. The Lord works the cross and the narrow way out for you when you give your whole heart and life to Him. You don't have to figure it out, it is not complicated, it is very simple, and it is not too hard.

> *"**Come to Me, all who are weary and heavy-laden, and I will give you rest**. "Take My yoke upon you and learn from Me, for I am gentle and humble in heart, and YOU WILL FIND REST FOR YOUR SOULS. "**For My yoke is easy and My burden is light**.* "(Matt. 11:28–30)

Manmade religion, with its many traditions, denominations, rituals, ceremonies, special days, religious superstitions, special meetings, expensive buildings, large budgets, paid staff, hired pastors, countless programs, many varied doctrinal teachings, differing beliefs, contradicting positions, hypocritical members, immoral pastors, "Christian" television and radio broadcasting, etc., is what has become very complicated and is a heavy yoke.

When you take away the "sinner's prayer" and explain to someone that they have to connect with God from the heart and repent of sin, the way to life makes much more sense.

When you take away the need for having to go somewhere to worship at a set time in order to serve and please God, it becomes a lot simpler.

When you take away the lie of the tithe, serving God becomes simpler.

When you define true worship as a heart function and a lifestyle practiced every day, serving and pleasing God becomes even simpler.

When you take away the paid pastor and the paid staff to manage a church, it gets even simpler.

When you realize that the way is narrow and that only a few will enter and there is no longer a need for large, expensive buildings, it clearly becomes even simpler.

When the paid pastor, paid staff, expensive programs, expensive buildings, and complicated budgets are no longer needed to have a simple true church, then the walk with God becomes a lot simpler.

When you realize that grace saves you by instructing you to not sin or give into worldly desires, but directs you to live sensibly, righteously, and godly right now and that faith saves you when you actively obey God's Word (His grace), then salvation becomes much simpler. Then grace and faith become much easier to understand. The cross is not always easy, but it is always simple. Denial of sin is not always easy, but it is always simple.

When you realize that you are forgiven of sin only if you repent (stop doing it) of sin, it becomes very simple.

When you realize that a "sinner's prayer" will not save you, but repentance from sin and a wholehearted relationship and love for God will save you, salvation becomes much simpler.

When you come to the reality that God will destroy you if you rebel against Him after being saved, the fear of the Lord will come upon you and will go a long way to make it much easier to deny yourself of sin. This makes it much simpler, to know that sin is never acceptable and that it could jeopardize your hope for heaven by giving into temptation.

To realize that the rapture is not going to come and snatch you away from tribulation, trouble, and suffering makes it a lot simpler and easier to accept the fact that you must endure your cross to the end, overcome and depend on Jesus only to be saved.

But be sure that I am not suggesting that you can save yourself. It takes two parts, your part and God's part. In my work, I sometimes had to use a product called two-part epoxy that came in two separate tubes. As long as either part remained in its own tube, each one remained soft and unchanged. But if you mixed an equal amount of each tube together, it quickly became hardened into a new substance similarly as hard and strong as most metals. This is a picture of how it works with our salvation. We can't save ourselves. Our part is useless without God's part. We can't do God's part and He won't do our part for us. But if we join ourselves with God, then we become a new creation and the two parts working together result in a strong and durable relationship with all the potential to overcome sin and endure to the end.

> *"**Abide in Me, and I in you**. As the branch cannot bear fruit of itself unless it abides in the vine, so **neither can you unless you abide in Me**. "I am the vine, you are the branches; he who abides in Me and I in him, he bears much fruit, **for apart from Me you can do nothing**. "If anyone does not abide in Me, he is thrown away as a branch and dries up; and they gather them, and cast them into the fire and they are burned.* (John 15:4–6)

Two things are perfectly clear here. First, you are required to bear the right kind of fruit in order to be saved and doing that is impossible unless you are in Jesus. So it takes both you and Jesus to bear the right fruit. You can't do it on your own and He won't do it for you. The second thing is if you don't choose to bear fruit while in Jesus, then Jesus will cut you off from the vine (Himself) and cast you into the fire (hell) to be burned. This proves that one can be in Jesus (saved) and still not obey the grace of God sent to him and end up lost forever.

That is simple. Get connected to Jesus and bear fruit or be cut off and burned up.

So how do you get connected to Jesus, the vine?

First, *you* must seek God in order to find Him. No one else can do this for you.

> *Sow with a view to righteousness, Reap in accordance with kindness; **Break up your fallow ground, For it is time to seek the Lord** Until He comes to rain **righteousness** on you.* (Hos. 10:12)

> *"**But seek first His kingdom and His righteousness**; and all these things shall be added to you."* (Matt. 6:33)

> *"**Ask**, and it shall be given to you; **seek**, and you shall find; **knock**, and it shall be opened to you."* (Matt. 7:7)

> *"If you then, being evil, know how to give good gifts to your children, how much more will your heavenly Father **give the Holy Spirit to those who ask Him**?"* (Luke 11:13)

So in your repentance and brokenness, cry out to God to save you and to reveal Himself to you by His Spirit. Draw near to Him in prayer and repentance asking for His mercy and His Holy Spirit.

> *But He gives a greater grace. Therefore it says, "GOD IS OPPOSED TO THE PROUD, BUT GIVES GRACE TO THE HUMBLE." Submit therefore to God. Resist the devil and he will flee from you **Draw near to God and He will draw near to you**. Cleanse your hands, you sinners; and purify your hearts, you double-minded. Be miserable and mourn and weep; let your laughter be turned into mourning and your joy to gloom. Humble yourselves in the presence of the Lord, and He will exalt you.* (Jas. 4:6–10)

As you draw near to God, He will draw near to you, but you must be willing to submit yourself to Him completely. Don't be half-hearted or lukewarm here. Get serious about this. Let your light-hearted religion be turned into gloom and start mourning over your double-minded belief that you could go to heaven while you live like the rest of the world. Humble yourself now and God will exalt you later.

In seeking God, you should be seeking for Him to save you, for the rebirth, to be born again by the Spirit so you can truly become free of sin, free of false religion and able to walk holy before the Lord.

You must be born again, born form above, born of the Holy Spirit—made new again!

> *Jesus answered, "Truly, truly, I say to you, unless one is born of water and the Spirit he cannot enter into the kingdom of God. "That which is born of the flesh is flesh, and that which is born of the Spirit is spirit. "Do not be amazed that I said to you, 'You must be born again.' "The wind blows where it wishes and you hear the sound of it, but do not know where it comes from and where it is going; so is everyone who is born of the Spirit."* (John 3:5–8)

So you must be born again by the Spirit of God. You cannot do this for yourself, it must be done by God. So what will it take to move God to cause you to be born again?

> *"Come to Me, all who are weary and heavy-laden, and I will give you rest. "Take My yoke upon you and learn from Me, for I am gentle and humble in heart, and YOU WILL FIND REST FOR YOUR SOULS. "For My yoke is easy and My burden is light."* (Matt. 11:28–30)

> *Jesus said to him, "I am the way, and the truth, and the life; no one comes to the Father but through Me.* (John 14:6)

*Jesus answered and said to him, "Truly, truly, I say to you, **unless one is born again he cannot see the kingdom of God**." (John 3:3)*

Run to Jesus. Cry out for Jesus. Seek for Jesus. He is the only way to the Father in heaven!

The one who is born again will be a new creation. His life and direction will be radically changed. He will be transformed into a new person. He is not just the same old person on the inside while wearing church going clothes on the outside, carrying a Bible and going to church. He is different and anyone who really knows him can see it. It will be obvious.

Therefore if anyone is in Christ, he is a new creature; the old things passed away; behold, new things have come. (2 Col. 5:17)

The one who is born again, does not sin as he did before. This is one of key marks of a true believer, the one who is born again. He does not practice/commit sin.

*Everyone who practices sin also practices lawlessness; and sin is lawlessness. You know that He appeared in order to take away sins; and in Him there is no sin. No one who abides in Him sins; no one who sins has seen Him or knows Him. Little children, make sure no one deceives you; the one who practices righteousness is righteous, just as He is righteous; the one who practices sin is of the devil; for the devil has sinned from the beginning. The Son of God appeared for this purpose, to destroy the works of the devil. **No one who is born of God practices sin**, because His seed abides in him; and he cannot sin, because he is born of God. By this the children of God and the children of the* *devil are obvious: anyone who does not practice righteousness is not of God, nor the one who does not love his brother.* (1 John 3:4–10)

Again, it is simple. If you see someone who is practicing/committing sin, he is a child of the devil. It doesn't matter if he is the pastor, Sunday school teacher or sings in the choir. On the other hand, if you see someone who does not practice sin, who is opposed to sin, who confronts so-called "Christians" who sin, who has the fear of God, then you know he is a true believer who is born again. Very, very simple.

So you cannot just decide that you are going to be born again. You need to find the Lord. He is the only one who can cause you to be born again. It is a miraculous work of the Holy Spirit. It is done for those who earnestly seek God and come to Him in distress, regret, sorrow and repentance for their sin and past rebellion against Him. When God sees this kind of heart and sincerity in you, He will have compassion on you and He will cause you to be born again. This is nothing like making a so-called "decision" for Christ, but a tremendous and powerful experience only brought about by the power of God when He sees the right kind of heart crying out to Him for mercy and for forgiveness. He never rejects the broken and contrite heart who is deeply grieved over his sin and who wants to change his ways.

> *For You do not delight in sacrifice, otherwise I would give it; You are not pleased with burnt offering.* **_The sacrifices of God are a broken spirit; A broken and a contrite heart, O God, You will not despise_**. (Ps. 51:16–17)

So coming to a deep sense of regret with a new determination to turn away from your sins and to turn to the Lord is very important to being born again. This is called repentance, the turning away from sin and turning toward God. But you must be sincere and wholehearted, or God will know the difference between a godly sorrow and a worldly sorrow.

> *Then He opened their minds to understand the Scriptures, and He said to them, "Thus it is written, that the Christ would suffer and rise again from the dead the third day, and **that repentance for forgiveness of sins** would be proclaimed in His name to all the nations, beginning from Jerusalem.* (Luke 24:45–47)

So repentance from sins is the only way to bring about forgiveness of sins. This is obviously the main key thing that will move God to forgive you and to cause you to be reborn by His Spirit.

> *"For I have no pleasure in the death of anyone who dies," declares the Lord GOD. "**Therefore, repent and live**."* (Ezek. 18:32)

Your repentance is not about making a simple apology to the Lord or an admission of sin, but is a heart wrenching conviction of sin filled with regret and shame, broken and taking all the blame for your sins. When you neither present excuses, nor blame anyone else for your sin and are truly sorry and want to be free from your sins, then you have the Lord's attention and He will respond and forgive you and save you by causing you to be born again by His Spirit.

Repentance is more than just realizing you are a sinner, but a wholehearted willingness to turn from your sins and to turn toward God and give up your life to God completely.

> *Then Jesus said to His disciples, "If anyone wishes to come after Me, he must deny himself, and take up his cross and follow Me. "**For whoever wishes to save his life will lose it; but whoever loses his life for My sake will find it**.* (Matt. 16:24–25)

So God knows your heart, your motives and your willingness to give up your life or not. If you are not sincere, then the Spirit of the Lord will not come near you, but another spirit will, a spirit of religion. Satan will offer you a simple "sinners prayer" and tell you that you are saved.

*Simon Peter, a bond-servant and apostle of Jesus Christ, To those who have received a faith of the same kind as ours, by the righteousness of our God and Savior, Jesus Christ: Grace and peace be multiplied to you in the knowledge of God and of Jesus our Lord; **seeing that His divine power has granted to us everything pertaining to life and godliness, through the true knowledge of Him who called us by His own glory and excellence**. For by these He has granted to us His precious and magnificent promises, so that by them you may become partakers of the divine nature, having escaped the corruption that is in the world by lust. Now for this very reason also, applying all diligence, in your faith supply moral excellence, and in your moral excellence, knowledge, and in your knowledge, self-control, and in your self-control, perseverance, and in your perseverance, godliness, and in your godliness, brotherly kindness, and in your brotherly kindness, love. For if these qualities are yours and are increasing, they render you neither useless nor unfruitful in the true knowledge of our Lord Jesus Christ. For he who lacks these qualities is blind or short-sighted, having forgotten his purification from his former sins. **Therefore, brethren, be all the more diligent to make certain about His calling and choosing you; for as long as you practice these things, you will never stumble; for in this way the entrance into the eternal kingdom of our***

Lord and Savior Jesus Christ will be abundantly supplied to you. (2 Pet. 1:1–11)

Now, if you have received the Spirit of the Lord through the rebirth, then you have these precious and magnificent promises. Everything pertaining to life and godliness has been granted to you. Everything means everything. You did your part so far by giving up your life to the Lord, and now He is doing his part by granting you everything pertaining to life and godliness. Again, this works in two parts. Grace has now instructed you to apply all diligence, faith, moral excellence, knowledge, self-control, perseverance, godliness, brotherly kindness, and love. Of course, all these qualities are God's, His divine nature, and when you are hooked to the vine (Jesus) you have the power to tap into them and practice them.

The promise goes on to say that if these qualities are yours and are increasing, that they render you neither useless nor unfruitful, and if you lack these qualities, that you are blind and have forgotten your purification of your former sins. Also, he said to be all the more diligent to make certain about His calling and choosing you. You see, everybody tells you to accept Christ, but the truth is that He must choose and accept you. To make certain that He does, keep doing what is right. For as long as you practice these things, you will never stumble and in this way the entrance into the eternal kingdom of our Lord and Savior Jesus Christ will be abundantly supplied to you. This is the gospel in a nutshell.

The true church is made up of truly born-again Christians. They are very rare today in America. Since there are so few, if you now are born again, you will have trouble finding anyone to fellowship with. If it is no one but you and the Lord, it is enough, but if you can find just one or two true believers to fellowship with, then you are even more blessed.

In Matthew 18:20, Jesus said, *"For where two or three have gathered together in My name, I am there in their midst."*

This is a picture of a true church; a few sincere people meeting together to seek God, study the Word of God and to teach and encourage one another to love God and walk with God until the end. There may be only two or three or a few more meeting in homes. Or maybe even enough to have to rent a small building to gather together for meetings. The church structure is always simple, no paid staff, no paid pastors, no executive offices, no expensive buildings, no special programs, no ministers of music, no choir or choir practice, no building programs, no big budgets, no tithes collected, no rituals or ceremonies, no worship service, no weird or strange practices, no one wearing robes, no steeples, no traditions of men, no false teachings, no excuses for sin and no nonsense.

You see, I have tried to make the way simple for you. It is a narrow way and the gate is small. As I have already explained, this narrow, small way is somewhat difficult. It is the way of suffering, rejection, self-denial, the cross, repentance, and only a few will find it. But it is not too difficult. Are you willing to be one of the few? Are you willing to seek God with all your heart or do you just want to join some church doing the easy thing and sit there until you die and go to hell? Do you love your religion more than God? Do you love son or daughter, mother or father, brother or sister more than God? Do you love your denominational doctrines more than God? Do you love your religious rituals and ceremonies more than God? Do you love your sin more than God? If you love anything more than God, you will never have Him or heaven.

If you are one of the typical American "Christians" that just play church and continue to live in sin and worldliness, then I hope you wake up from your sleep and repent from all your idolatry, worldly pleasures and ungodliness and stop pretending to be a Christian but instead be broken and ashamed for all your hypocrisy. In your shame, I hope the fear of the Lord will come upon you and that you run toward the Lord in repentance, so you can be saved by truly being born again. See if what Jesus said below speaks to you:

"To the angel of the church in Laodicea (like America) *write: The Amen, the faithful and true*

*Witness, the Beginning of the creation of God, says this: 'I know your deeds, that you are neither cold nor hot; I wish that you were cold or hot. '**So because you are lukewarm, and neither hot nor cold, I will spit you out of My mouth**. 'Because you say, "I am rich, and have become wealthy, and have need of nothing," and you do not know that you are wretched and miserable and poor and blind and naked, I advise you to buy from Me gold refined by fire so that you may become rich, and white garments so that you may clothe yourself, and that the shame of your nakedness will not be revealed; and eye salve to anoint your eyes so that you may see. '**Those whom I love, I reprove and discipline; therefore be zealous and repent**. 'Behold, I stand at the door and knock; if anyone hears My voice and opens the door, I will come in to him and will dine with him, and he with Me. 'He who overcomes, I will grant to him to sit down with Me on My throne, as I also overcame and sat down with My Father on His throne. '**He who has an ear, let him hear what the Spirit says to the churches**.'''*
(Rev. 3:14–22)

Are you not sick of this false American "Christian" religion yet? Are you going to do anything about your soul? Are you willing to be rejected and persecuted by your church friends and family for taking a stand for the truth? Are you willing to take the heat when you reject the myths that have been exposed in this book and the many more "Christian myths" you will discover if you study the Bible? Are you willing to give yourself completely to the Lord? Are you willing to turn from all your sin and to walk with the Lord faithfully until the end of your life? If not, why not? Do you still trust in myths to save you? Jesus once asked, _"What will a man give in exchange for his soul?"_ Sadly, the answer really is, not very much. A little sin, a little religion, a little idol, that is all it takes. What about you? Will you trade your eternal soul for something so small, so petty, so worthless in view of eternity or will you turn to the Lord and give up your life now, so you will find life for all eternity? What will it be, life or death? May you choose life today before it is too late!

Don Britton
Chrisianmyths.org@gmail.com
www.Christianmyths.org

About the Author

I am now seventy years of age. I have walked with God for thirty-eight-plus years. I have seriously studied the Scriptures all that time. I am very concerned about the American "Christian" church world. So many people are deceived. So many people don't seek God. So many people are in sin while they think they are going to heaven. So many people don't study the Scriptures, but just go by whatever the pastor tells them. So many pastors are just leading by repetition learned from traditions passed down to them, without taking any serious concern for the souls and the lives of the people. Therefore, so many people are going to hell and don't even know it.

The purpose of this book is to try to stimulate people to seek God through study and prayer, so they might be a part of the very few who will be saved. I hope that many people will wake up before it is too late. I hope you find the truth and discover peace with God. Don't trust any man but study the Scriptures for yourself. It is everyone's personal responsibility to find the truth for themselves, and no one can pay any man (pastor) to do that for them. Jesus said, "If you abide in my Word, then you would know the truth and the truth would set you free." May you abide in His word and know the truth for yourself and then you will be free and free indeed!

Sincerely,
Don Britton